THE
edible front yard

THE
edible front yard

The Mow-Less, Grow-More Plan for a Beautiful, Bountiful Garden

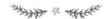

by IVETTE SOLER

with photographs by ANN SUMMA

TIMBER PRESS

Portland / London

PREVIOUS PAGE: A monochromatic hedge of French lavender and globe thistle gives an ornamental backbone to this edible front yard. Photo by Ann Summa

The Haseltine Building
133 S.W. Second Avenue, Suite 450
Portland, Oregon 97204-3527
www.timberpress.com

2 The Quadrant
135 Salusbury Road
London NW6 6RJ
www.timberpress.co.uk

DESIGNED by Cat Grishaver
FRONT COVER ILLUSTRATION © Lorena Siminovich
GARDEN DESIGN ILLUSTRATIONS by Marjorie C. Leggitt and Cat Grishaver
PRINTED in China
SECOND PRINTING 2011

Library of Congress Cataloging-in-Publication Data
Soler, Ivette.
  The edible front yard : the mow-less, grow-more plan for a beautiful, bountiful garden / Ivette Soler ; with photographs by Ann Summa. -- 1st ed.
     p. cm.
  "Foreword by Fritz Haeg."
  Includes bibliographical references and index.
  ISBN 978-1-60469-199-3
  1. Edible landscaping. 2. Plants, Edible. 3. Gardens--Design. I. Summa, Ann.
II. Title.
  SB475.9.E35S65 2011
  635--dc22

A catalog record for this book is also available from the British Library.

table of contents

foreword

BY FRITZ HAEG

Ideas of beauty change with the times, and this book will guide you in the creation of a more evolved and exciting version of front yard beauty that prizes health, diversity, and pleasure over short-term convenience. A lawn is a lawn is a lawn is a lawn, always the same, boring, and conformist, but the garden adventure you are about to embark on is much more fun. These bountiful, dense, diverse, perhaps a bit eccentric, and even slightly wild edible gardens put us back in touch with the land that we live on, the people around us, and the food that we eat. This is a call to arms for you, the front yard gardener, to publicly create your own personal version of the American Dream for the twenty-first century.

The front lawn was the great symbol of the American Dream before we knew better. Connecting home to home from coast to coast, it was originally conceived as a common green. But now it has become clear that this wasteful time-consuming toxic monoculture occupying that critical space between the front door and street is actually an anti-social space, perhaps only occasionally inhabited by someone pushing a loud and polluting two-stroke motor back and forth. The custom of the front lawn has consumed the American landscape with the idea that it was convenient. But just how convenient is a space that takes so much and gives us so little in return? Now that we understand the social and environmental costs of this purely ceremonial space, how can we possibly consider it beautiful?

Are you brave enough to step out your front door and rip up your lawn? Are you creative enough to plan a new garden that will be on view for all of your neighbors to see? Do you know enough to be able to select the right plants and prepare the beds for them to thrive? Are you dedicated enough to do the daily work necessary to publicly grow your own food? This is a down and dirty how-to book, and by picking it up, you have already demonstrated that you are not just interested in reading about this radical act of gardening, but actually doing it. This book will provide you with enough courage, ideas, and information to confidently stride out that front door and get started.

Fritz Haeg is the author of *Edible Estates.*

OPPOSITE: Bronze fennel tickles its neighbors: an artichoke and the colorful 'Sticks on Fire' euphorbia. Photo by Ann Summa

preface

A front yard revolution is at our fingertips and on our doorsteps. Its time has come. **Walking through the ethnically diverse neighborhoods of East Los Angeles, I am always struck by the fascinating and creative ways people utilize their front yards. Some communities are dotted with front yard farms bursting with fruit trees, sugar cane, melons, brassicas, and all manner of greens in well-tended rows, along with pass-along plants from family members. The traditional front yard—the useless, boring, out-dated lawn adorned by a few shade trees and perhaps some lackluster shrubbery—pales in comparison to these vibrant, productive spaces where growing food is serious business. I find these front yard farms inspirational; they speak to a resourcefulness that is long-gone in mainstream American culture, and they have a beauty all their own. Growing edibles out front is also a smart, practical choice: it takes advantage of the simple fact that wherever lawn can thrive—in places with significant amounts of sunshine—so too can herbs, fruits, and vegetables.**

While record numbers of people are growing food and returning to more thoughtful land and resource use, it's unlikely that strictly utilitarian front yard farms will be widely seen anytime soon. We still want our front yards to look like gardens. We still want the front of our house to be an inviting and livable space—an extension of ourselves and a reflection of our personal style. The challenge lies in weaving together the pieces to create a front yard that is sustainable, beautifully designed, *and* edible: a modern-day victory garden. It can be done.

When I purchased my home, I promptly ripped out the front lawn and planted a garden that included such drought-tolerant plants as sages, grasses, and succulents. My blossoming as a cook followed this transformation and I slowly began integrating tough herbs (culinary sages, marjoram, and basils) and architectural edibles, like artichokes and fennel, to associate with the bold agaves that dominate my public garden. Without sacrificing my strong, sculptural planting style, I now have glorious herbs to cook with and vegetables to eat almost all year long. The creation of my successful, interesting, rewarding garden took years, but equipped with the right information, you can have it much faster than I did.

This book will show you how to create the new front yard: a diverse, sustainable mix of ornamentals and edibles, imaginatively designed and organically gardened. The process starts by taking a step back—looking at what inspires you—to hone in on the particular style of curb appeal you want to cultivate. Next comes the ornamental edibles: a plant palette of statement-makers and super-models, from exotic plants, like paddle cactus, to garden standbys that you may not have realized were even edible (rose hip tea, anyone?). The shrubs, trees, and perennials in the palette of helpers (many of which are edible in their own right) will help you create a garden with year-round interest to spare. Armed with enough plants choices to fill your garden a hundred times over—and the principles of structure, repetition, form, texture, and color discussed in the design primer—the possibilities for breathtaking ornamental combinations are endless. From there, it's reality time: look at what you have, see the lawn you want to remove, decide what you hardscape you want to build. And then take the methods in this book and do it. Get your dream garden out of your mind and into the front yard—your organic, homegrown, delicious food won't be far behind.

The heart of this revolution goes much deeper than the visible surface. By minimizing your lawn, you are taking a stand against turfgrass as the biggest irrigated crop in America. You are saying no to something that takes precious resources without giving back anything just as precious. Growing food in your front yard is a courageous expression: you are telling people that you care about what your family eats. You are also setting an example for your neighbors. Are you the type of person who can be the standard bearer for a new kind of garden? Be bold and brave, because no matter who you are, there is a style of edible planting that will capture your imagination and suit your taste—from the wildly mixed and exuberant to the elegant and composed.

Growing food can be integrated into our daily lives. And such a fundamental change can be reflected in our front yards, for everyone to enjoy and admire. Let's make this happen!

OPPOSITE, TOP: This front yard in Napa, California, is what a front yard could be. Photo by Rebecca Sweet. Garden of Freeland and Sabrina Tanner

OPPOSITE, BOTTOM: An edible front yard in Seattle, Washington. Photo by Ann Summa. Garden design by Chris Saleeba of Fresh Digs

acknowledgments

This book would not have come together without the clear vision and constant belief of Juree Sondker, who is a writer's dream. She and Mollie Firestone (who was given a puzzle and found a book in it) are the best editors anyone could ask for.

Fritz Haeg, you are an inspiration. I am humbled by your grace and generosity. You are without a doubt the KING of the edible front yard.

To all the Facebook followers of "Front Yard Food": thank you for the fun, the chats, and the cross talk. We are garden fiends, each and every one of us. Your input and insight was (and is) invaluable.

To my blogfriends: Debra Lee Baldwin, Andrea Bellamy, Shirley Bovshow, Willi Galloway, Jayme Jenkins, Alice Joyce, Adriana Martinez, Susan Morrison, Pam Penick, Jenny Nybro Peterson, Christina Salwitz, Laura Livengood Schaub, and Rebecca Sweet—you are my sisters. Thank you for your support, advice, and good cheer. We all get satin tour jackets.

Carla Denker, Kevin Hanley, Judy Kameon, Michael Kirchman, Jr., Tom Marble, and Pae White— your friendship and enthusiastic support means the world to me.

To Carlos Sosa, my fabulous and talented little brother—we've come a long way. Let's keep going!

Those who contributed to and appeared in the book— Laura Cooper, Nick Taggart, and Lily Cooper-Taggart; Shawna Coronado; Erik Knutzen and Kelly Coyne; Theresa Loe; Yvette Roman and Fred Davis; Chris, Ashley, and Lola Saleeba; Laura Livengood Schaub; Rebecca Sweet; Pae White and Tom Marble—thank you all for opening your gardens to us and for holding off harvesting.

Ann Summa, my photographer and friend, there aren't words . . .

Zac Montanaro and William Kaminski—you are my heroes.

And finally, to my best friend, soul mate, and big love, Jan Tumlir: thanks for going on this roller coaster ride with me and not jumping off!

OPPOSITE: Growing our own food is a precious gift we give to the ones we love most. Photo by Ann Summa

one

INSPIRED CURB APPEAL

Let's face it—not many neighborhoods will be friendly to a no-holds-barred edible landscape. **Economics is among the most pressing reasons for this since your property value is intertwined with the property values of your neighbors. If you do anything that might adversely affect the perceived or assessed value of your home, such as neglecting your property, using your yard as alternative parking for your cars, or planting a raucous farm out front, there is bound to be some pushback. Don't forget about the power of curb appeal; a great looking front yard garden is a wonderful asset to your home. Why not plant your food with an eye toward the overall beauty of your front yard? I suggest a gentler approach to creating an edible garden in such a prominent location: integrate. Integrating fruits, vegetables, and herbs with ornamentals is the best way to approach a garden that has the extra demand upon it to look great all year long. By expanding our edible palette, we create pleasing planting associations that help our edible gardens look the best they can throughout the seasons. These gardens will literally stop traffic.**

beauty matters

Anything you grow in your front yard has to work hard for you. You want that prime piece of real estate to look fantastic as well as perform for you throughout the seasons, so any edible you plant there is under extra pressure. It will be scrutinized. When dealing with the front of your home, we have to come to grips with the fact that beauty matters. Your front yard is a greeting to the world.

Before jumping into creating your new front yard edible garden, take some time to think about what you are about to do. It'll be fun, but you *are* going public. When your vegetable garden is in the backyard, you have the freedom to "let it all hang out." But out front you need to make deliberate choices that give your edibles as much ornamental appeal as any well-designed garden. This involves getting to know the vegetables, herbs, and fruits that give you not only the food you want, but also the ease of care you need and the good looks you crave.

The successful edible front yard garden all comes down to the right plant in the right place. We have to be brutally selective, following the same kind of rules used by ornamental gardeners, when choosing which edibles to plant out front. Yes, these extra generous plants do us the honor of feeding us, but when they are placed front and center they have another set of standards they need to meet. Here are my criteria for any edible plant to be included in a front yard garden.

....

PREVIOUS PAGE, TOP: A front yard doesn't need a lawn to be beautiful. In this garden, thyme and rosemary carpet the ground, and artichokes mingle with perennials to create a harmonious and productive balance. Garden design and photo by Laura Livengood Schaub.

PREVIOUS PAGE, BOTTOM: A red nasturtium and the florescent stems of ruby chard. Photo by Ann Summa

OPPOSITE: The glowing purple tones of artichoke flowers hardly need help to shine, but when placed against a backdrop of magenta bougainvillea, the effect is stunning. Photo by Ann Summa

RULES FOR FRONT YARD EDIBLES

1. The entire plant must have a pleasing form—it cannot stand on the merits of its flowers (or vegetable or fruit) alone.

2. It has to give me at least two reasons to plant it (such as color and form, or texture and seedpods).

3. Its leaves must hold up for the entire growing season. Some edibles have leaves that are susceptible to mildews, or are such heavy feeders that the foliage is just worn out by the end of the season. In the backyard, you can deal with it. In the front yard, plant something else.

4. If you must plant less ornamental edibles in the front yard because you have no other suitable space, pay extra attention to your hardscape. It's a lot easier to overlook wilted cucumber leaves if they are supported by a beautiful trellis.

style

Everyone has a style: some of us are casual while others live to preen and have all eyes upon them. Gardens are no different, especially when they are in the front yard. By choosing to create an edible garden in public view, you are telling people quite a bit about yourself. Are you an organized, hardcore food devotee who has grown your own fruits and vegetables for years? Your front yard should reflect your knowledge and passion, and you should invest in an infrastructure (what we in the garden design business call *hardscape*—raised beds, paths, patios, and trellises) that will make your garden as lovely as it is productive. Or maybe you are new to gardening but you want to have it all—an eclectic garden that feeds your eye as well as your family. You can integrate herbs, fruits, and vegetables into your ornamental plantings and create a fun, hybrid mix of garden styles.

Your choices will be apparent to your neighbors and to all who pass by. If you make those choices carefully you will create a front yard food garden with style and flair.

SO WHAT IS STYLE?

All the choices you've made throughout your life—where you live, what you wear, what movies you like, whether you own a dog or a cat—add up to your style. You may not be aware of your style, but other people are. A large part of any design process is identifying style and figuring out how to translate it, and a good first step is to take a look at the things you love.

At the beginning of a project, designers will gather images, swatches, and small items that catch their eye. Patterns or repetitions of themes, colors, and ideas that emerge during this process will often influence or direct the design. It is hard to visualize a project completely in your head. At some point you'll need to start seeing your inspiration in one place so that you can begin to focus on what's working and what isn't. A mood board is a simple tool used by designers in all different media—clothing, interiors, gardens, products—to help refine an idea into a concrete visual form.

where you dwell

The modern garden is a regional garden, especially when it's an edible front yard. Observing the specifics of your region with an open mind can bring a tremendous amount of richness to the beginning stages of a design process. Let the natural surroundings or the history of your state, county, or city be your muse.

We no longer want the front of our home to look like a yard in Anywhere, USA. Tap into your region's essential character—perhaps it is the classical, southern charm of Savannah, Georgia, or the eclectic, anything-goes attitude of San Francisco—and reflect that inspiration in the design of your edible garden. For example, in rough and tumble central Texas, aluminum stock tanks used by ranchers for feeding and watering cattle have been appropriated by gardeners. When these familiar objects are repurposed as raised beds, planters, and ponds, the look is beautifully grounded in place and says "Texas" loud and clear.

Your choice of plants can also speak volumes about your region. In Southern California, well-known for its citrus groves, a front yard lemon tree pays homage to an old Hollywood spirit almost as effectively as a palm

🌿 *mood board* 🌿

Creating a mood board is simple and fun. You can find out quite a lot about your style, what you are looking for in your garden, and how your ideas will work together.

Materials

- Magazines, fabric, photographs, and other items of interest
- A cork board
- Pins
- A photograph of your house

Steps

1. Collect anything that intrigues you: this is the time to stay open to all sources of inspiration. Peruse garden, fashion, shelter, and food-focused magazines. Gather photographs of plants, rocks, bricks, stones, or whatever catches your eye. Don't limit yourself to the one-dimensional. If a piece of fabric speaks to you, get a swatch of it. If you find a special gravel mix, put a handful in a ziplock bag. Even a troll doll with fuzzy hair can be a valuable piece of inspiration (yes, there are orange grasses that can perfectly mimic a troll doll's hair).

2. Hang the cork board on a wall that you see often and pin the picture of your house onto the board. Surround your house with the images, colors, textures, and other items that inspire you.

3. Keep changing things around as much as you want. Maybe the colors you thought you loved are too harsh. Or you'll notice an element that you want to focus on, like the texture of stone or the verdigris on your copper gutters. You might be able to incorporate a color or pattern from the fabric into your garden. Or the fabric may become an awning for your front windows—you never know.

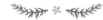

tree—and you get juicy fruit as a bonus. The state of Washington is rich with apple orchards, and eating crisp, delicious apples freshly picked from your front yard is a luxury that most climates can't provide. Be guided by the specifics of your region.

YOUR SIDE OF TOWN

Another step in this process is to take long walks around your neighborhood and carefully study the surrounding houses. Is your neighborhood uniformly planned with houses of similar color and architectural style? Or do you live in an area that is more eclectic? Take a look at how your neighbors have planted their front yards. If others have removed their lawns and replaced them with gardens, notice how those gardens use the space. You'll see that homes that have a mix of plants surrounding them seem more grounded, friendly, and interesting than those with the traditional lawn and foundation planting.

PLANTING FOR WHERE YOU LIVE

Look at the plants in your neighborhood and pay special attention to what is thriving. Easy-to-care-for gardens need plants that do well in your area. Don't discount plants even if they seem too common: there's no such thing as a bad plant, or an unfashionable plant, only a plant that hasn't been used well. Junipers, for example, are often considered dull and boring, but they can help create an evergreen rhythm to gardens in all parts of the country—hot or cold—and in all kinds of garden situations, from sunny to part shade. (Junipers also produce beautiful berries that can be used as spices in cooking and in herbal beverages—a natural partner to the front yard edible palette.)

While hobby gardeners will often hunt down and culti-vate plants from different climates, it is always smarter to choose plants that are accustomed to the area in which you live. The USDA zone map divides the country into eleven hardiness zones, each of which shows a dif-ferent area of minimum winter temperatures. Knowing what zone you live in will give you a good general idea of what plants will flourish in your area.

Visiting your local nursery and talking to the knowl-edgeable staff is a smart step to take before choosing plants. I have never met a staff member at a nursery who doesn't love talking about plants and the best way to grow them. They will know which fruit trees flour-ish where you live, if you need tomato varieties that will ripen early in cool weather, or what type of lettuce is best for hot weather. Not only is every zone different, but your particular city, side of town, or even neighbor-hood may have specific variables that affect the way your plants grow. Getting advice from someone who understands the way things grow in your climate can save you time and money.

the place you call home

Now that you've explored your environs and have seen what is happening plantwise in your neighborhood, take a good look at your house. When designing a garden in a front yard, the general style of the house tells me where to go. I often contrast the style of garden with the style of the house, but beautiful gardens can complement the style of a house as well. My definition of contemporary and traditional has more to do with the architectural approach rather than when the house was built. Let's figure out where your house falls in this spectrum.

CONTEMPORARY HOME

This broad-ranging term identifies a style of building that focuses on function rather than ornamentation. Building materials are used in a straightforward way. Clean lines and open spaces are emphasized. Natural light is utilized to its fullest potential, so these houses have large expanses of glass windows and sliding doors. A defined relationship often exists between the indoor and outdoor spaces; breezeways and overhangs are important exterior features. Most contemporary styled homes are either one-story or split-leveled. The ranch-style and mid-century modern homes are examples of contemporary architecture.

....

PREVIOUS PAGE: In many areas of the country, citrus are easy front yard trees. In the entry to the home of artist Pae White and architect Tom Marble, the vibrant yellow of the lemons activate the space with color. Even the pavers have yellow tumbled glass sprinkled in. Photo by Ivette Soler

OPPOSITE: A little research will help you find the plants that grow best in the area you live, like thyme in Southern California. Photo by Ann Summa

Often, the indoor/outdoor characteristics of a contemporary home allow for a certain amount of interaction between the plantings and the architecture, such as the opportunity for planting under a breezeway, or maybe even creating a garden of thyme on a green roof. Since contemporary houses tend to have clean lines and defined edges, I like to contrast them with bold, big, raucous gardens that play against their streamlined nature. Dramatic plants look fantastic in the gardens of modern houses, as does an emphatic use of hardscape. Building raised beds? Think about building ten of them, with one crop in each bed. Use the simplicity of your contemporary home as a strength in your landscape design.

TRADITIONAL HOME

Traditional houses aren't necessarily older, they just look that way. It's a matter of ornamentation. Windows are smaller and more numerous, there might be pillars or porticos, columns or shutters, peaked or gabled roofs. There tends to be more symmetry, with the front door as the focus of the façade and a walkway that leads from the door to a sidewalk or driveway. Colonial, Tudor, Italianate, and Victorian are all examples of traditional architecture. Many new houses are built to mimic these styles—our suburbs are full of neo-traditional homes. They can be one-story bungalows or two-story clapboard houses but they all have the familiar feel of an all-American home.

Gardens that complement a traditional house often focus on creating a sense of the familiar and the comfortable. A front yard edible garden feels appropriate to these homes, many of which reflect time periods when victory gardens were de rigueur. Fountains, pottery, and other personal touches are pleasing in a traditional front yard edible garden. I also find these houses well suited to formal treatments, such as small hedges bordering the planting beds or decorative arbors for scarlet runner beans to crawl over. The overall effect will be one of charm and grace.

....

OPPOSITE, TOP The angles and clean lines of these raised beds make them an excellent choice for the front yard edible garden of a house with a simple, contemporary appeal. Photo by Ann Summa. Garden of Laura Cooper and Nick Taggart

OPPOSITE, BOTTOM: A small front lawn surrounded by a charming cottage-style planting of edibles and perennials. This is the neo-traditional home of Theresa Loe, a garden educator and communicator. Photo by Ann Summa

two

THE NEW FRONT YARD PLANT PALETTE

the ornamental edibles

We are so lucky these days. **The gardener who wants a flair-filled edible garden has a vast array of plant choices that would be welcome in any garden, anywhere: from fantastic heirloom vegetables and herbs from other cultures to newly cultivated varieties selected by growers with an eye to ornamental appeal. A warning to vegetable fanatics (among whose ranks I count myself). Some edibles do not appear in this book—in fact, I might skip some of your favorites. While hardcore food growers might argue that any plant that nourishes and sustains is inherently beautiful, some fruits, herbs, and vegetables are simply not the best choices for an edible garden with an ornamental focus. Some have leaves that are prone to disease or just don't look as sprightly once the fruiting body has set. Others are complicated to grow: asparagus, for example, requires trenching and years of work before food can be harvested.**

An attractive front yard edible garden will win many more converts to the cause of homegrown food. This section showcases plants that will put their best face forward while performing their hearts out. For surefire panache in your edible front yard, be certain to lean on the supermodels of the ornamental edible plant world. Explore the different cultivars and use them to create unique visual and textural combinations in your garden.

the supermodels

- Artichokes
- Basil
- Beans
- Chard
- Corn
- Eggplants
- Kale
- Lettuce
- Peppers
- Sage

PREVIOUS PAGE: Well-chosen edibles such as red looseleaf lettuce and pole beans with twining purple stems can have a powerful, eye-pleasing presence in your front yard. Photo by Ann Summa

OPPOSITE, TOP: Chard is such an eye-catching plant that many grow it for its ornamental appeal alone. Photo by Rebecca Sweet

OPPOSITE, BOTTOM: Even in a garden this dramatic, the sight of amaranth in bloom can steal the scene. Photo by Ann Summa. Garden of Laura Cooper and Nick Taggart

AMARANTH
Amaranthus tricolor

Annual; foliage and flowers run the colorful gamut from green to gold to purple to red; late summer bloom; 3 ft. high × 2 ft. wide.

Amaranth is known primarily as a grain, but it is also cultivated around the world for its leaves. Its extraordinary beauty makes it a slam-dunk for inclusion in front yard edible gardens. Different varieties come in a glorious rainbow of colors—shades of red, purple, gold, and green—and the flowers always coordinate with the leaves. The burgundy selections are my favorite: the deep ruby young leaves hold their color when cooked and the flowers have a fantastic texture as well as tint. While it is tempting to eat all the tender leaves, let some of your amaranth plants bloom into highly textural, furry flowers.

How to grow it: Amaranth loves heat: give it sun and not too much water and it will thrive. This plant is for anyone who loves their beauties tough as nails—amaranth will grow in a sidewalk crack and still turn heads. Annual in all zones.

How to use it: Sauté the leaves and add them to salads —think of it as summer spinach. You can also try growing a swath of it and letting it blossom; when the blossoms are still tight, harvest the seeds by drying the flowers in a low oven, and then store the seeds in an airtight container. Roast the seeds, add them to hot or cold cereal, and consider yourself a front yard breakfast pioneer.

APPLE
Malus domestica

....

Deciduous tree; green leaves; five-petaled flowers from creamy white to shell pink to rosy red; mainly early summer bloom; size varies from dwarf to standard.

....

Who doesn't love an apple? Growing apples at home is very rewarding—the high levels of chemical residue in commercially grown apples will be completely absent from your organic ones. A wide assortment of dwarf and semi-dwarf trees will fit into a front yard without sacrificing too much garden space. When in bloom, apple trees are beautiful, and a tree heavy with apples is emblematic of a good harvest season.

How to grow it: Be sure to choose varieties that are resistant to disease, such as *Malus domestica* 'Liberty' and 'William's Pride'; our front yard edibles, especially our trees, should be tough and beautiful. Even if you don't have a lot of space, you can still grow these fantastic trees espaliered against a fence; this old technique directs the growth of branches to be flat against a surface without sacrificing fruiting potential. Those of us in the hotter zones of the United States might not be able to grow as many varieties as our northern friends, but explore—there are more choices than you might think. And those of you in zones 3–8, rejoice!

How to use it: Pies, applesauce, cider, sautéed with pork chops—the list goes on and on. The real question is, what *can't* you use apples in? You can also enjoy an early burst of spring by "forcing" an apple branch to bloom indoors. By late winter, most apple varieties have broken dormancy and are ready to be forced. Cut a long, straight branch that has many visible growth nodes and bring it inside. Smash the bottom of the branch with a hammer (this allows it to draw up more water), place the branch in a vase of lukewarm water, and leave it in a bright, cool place for three to four weeks. When your apple branch blooms, you'll feel like you've made magic.

....

OPPOSITE: Luscious apples look as crisp and cool as a day in the Pacific Northwest. Photo by Ivette Soler

how to espalier

When you espalier a fruit tree, you guide it to grow flat against a wall, fence, or support structure. **This is a classic technique that can save room in your edible garden and create a feature that is as elegant as it is useful. Don't be afraid of fancy pruning—the steps are straightforward and the hardest thing is making the first cut. You will be amazed at how easy and rewarding it is to artfully prune your fruit trees. You can go easy and espalier your tree so that it simply sits flat against a wall and looks natural from the front. Or you can make patterns with the branches that elevate your apples, pears, or plums to sculpture. An espaliered tree will not only be exceptionally pleasing to the eye, but the fruit it produces will be bigger, sweeter, and juicier.**

These instructions are for a two-tiered apple tree that will grow flat against a 3 ft. tall front yard fence. It is easier to do this type of espalier with a small tree that already has some side branching. Don't make it more difficult by getting a large tree that will need extensive pruning to espalier into this shape. Starting with a bare root fruit tree or a 5-gal. specimen would be the best choice.

Materials

- One dwarf apple tree appropriate to your zone
- Measuring tape
- Pencil to mark measurements
- Drill
- Eyehooks
- Heavy gauge wire
- Compost
- Pruning shears
- Ties to hold branches in place (buy these at garden centers or use old strips of ripped nylon hose)

Steps: setting your wire guides

1. Decide on your center, which is where the trunk will eventually be. Measure 18 in. from the soil line—this is where your first tier of branches will be. That point will also be the center of a 48 in. horizontal wire support.

2. Using that center point, measure and mark 24 in. to the left and 24 in. to the right—this represents the 48 in. of branching.

3. Drill holes every 8 in. along the 48 in. branch line for your eyehooks. Insert your eyehooks, and then thread the heavy gauge wire through the eyehooks. Eventually the branches will be strong enough to support themselves but for the first few years they will need the help of the wire to support the mature fruit.

4. Go back to your center and measure up another 18 in. This will be the top tier of your fruit tree.

5. Repeat steps 2 and 3.

6. Return to your center mark and create a center vertical support by attaching a wire from the bottom horizontal tier to the top horizontal tier. This vertical wire will be the guide for the trunk of your espalier.

Steps: planting and pruning

1. Plant your tree on the center line and amend the hole well with compost.

2. If your tree already has side branches, trim them back to the trunk. If you are lucky enough to have selected a specimen that already has two branches at 18 in. (or in the near vicinity), gently guide them onto the first set of horizontal guide wires and tie them.

3. Take a deep breath. Cut the trunk 2 in. above the first set of guide wires. This will force horizontal growth below the cut. If you had no horizontal branches at 18 in., the buds of the tree will break and the side branches will begin to grow. If you already had branches, these will grow stronger.

4. Choose one of these fresh, flexible branches as the new "central leader" or trunk. Attach it to the vertical guide wire. As it grows upward, prune any side shoots. The only growth should be the first tier horizontal branches and the new trunk.

5. Once the trunk has grown above the second tier of supports, take another deep breath and cut it 2 in. above that point.

6. Once the branches start growing, select two to guide onto the wires and tie them gently. Prune all other side branches.

7. Once you have your structure in place, keep pruning to redirect growth to the four branches. Prune selectively so fruit will have maximum exposure to the sun.

NOTE: *If you decide to have a line of espaliered fruit trees against your fence, be sure to measure 48 in. from trunk to trunk.*

OPPOSITE: Neatly espaliered apple trees, trained flat against a wall or fence, can fit into the smallest edible front yard—even a large, multi-tiered specimen like this one. Photo by Ann Summa

ARTICHOKE
Cynara scolymus

....

Perennial often grown as an annual; large, gray to green, deeply incised leaves; unique purple blossom; upright fountain-like habit; summer bloom; 3–5 ft. tall and wide; 100–150 days to maturity.

....

The artichoke is the hands-down superstar of front yard food. This large, beautiful member of the thistle family has such a strong form that it can be part of your edible garden's backbone. The delicious "choke" is actually a flower that we harvest before it blossoms. It might be hard, but try and let some of your artichokes bloom. You will get one of the most unusual, delightful flowers in the plant kingdom—a luminous purple crew-cut sitting on top of a softball-sized globe that drives bees crazy. For all the wonder of the yummy choke and whimsical blossom, the leaves of the artichoke are what makes it so valuable in the front yard. The gray color acts as a foil for the green leaves of most edibles, and the strong, thick, serrated texture is incredibly eye-catching.

How to grow it: Artichokes are not reliably perennial for most of the country—if you are colder than zone 8 you can grow it as an annual and it will still give you delicious chokes from the first year. Make sure to start these big, heavy feeders with lots of rich compost mixed into the soil, and give them fish emulsion and/or worm tea throughout the season. Cut the bottom leaves as they begin to look ratty and add them to your compost. Once the chokes are harvested, refresh the plant by cutting it back to soil level. Hard pruning is scary, but you will be rewarded with new, unblemished foliage to light up your fall garden.

How to use it: Grill, steam, or broil—then dip it in your favorite sauce and enjoy. Don't forget those astonishing blossoms. Once the bees have had a pollen party, bring a bloom or two indoors as long-lasting cut flowers.

ARUGULA
Eruca sativa

....

Annual; green, deeply cut leaves; small, creamy white flowers with purple-striped petals; 12–18 in. tall × 12 in. wide; 45 days to maturity.

....

Arugula is as wonderful an addition to a garden as it is to a salad. The deeply cut leaves grow in green rosettes and the more you cut the more you'll get. If you let arugula flower you'll be rewarded by one of its best assets: a beautiful haze of creamy little blossoms that look and taste fantastic.

How to grow it: Sprinkle seed in lightly cultivated and amended soil and keep it moist until it germinates. Arugula loves to self-seed; allow it to go wherever it wants and you will have wonderful surprise plants that will enhance your garden and your kitchen. All the little arugula seedlings will give you the opportunity to weed it and eat it! Plant in early spring for a late spring to early summer harvest. Annual in all zones.

How to use it: Arugula has a magical way of making everything tastier. Use the peppery, nutty leaves in salads, as a bed for grilled meats, or to make pesto. Try the tasty flowers in sandwiches, as a garnish on bagels, or as a simple snack in the garden.

....

OPPOSITE, TOP LEFT: Arugula is always welcome, wherever in the garden it chooses to show up. Photo by Ivette Soler

OPPOSITE, TOP RIGHT: Let a few of your artichokes flower and craft a stunning cut-flower arrangement. Photo by Ivette Soler

OPPOSITE, BOTTOM: The mighty artichoke has it all—amazing leaves, beautiful color, bold form—and it's delicious. Photo by Ivette Soler

BACHELOR'S BUTTONS
Centaurea cyanus

Annual flower; green to gray foliage; white, blue, pink, or black flowers; upright and a bit rangy; early summer bloom; 24–30 in. tall × 8–16 in. wide; 80–95 days to maturity.

Of all the edible flowers, bachelor's buttons (*Centaurea cyanus*) may be my favorite. They pop up easily from scattered seed and fill in the inevitable gaps in a young garden. My top pick is *C. cyanus* 'Black Ball', a gorgeous maroon flower on a plant with steel gray leaves. Blue, white, and pink varieties are also available.

How to grow it: Bachelor's buttons are pleasantly easy to grow; start them from seed or buy plants in six packs from your local nursery. They are fast growers and do well in sunny or dappled conditions. Don't eat all the flowers—let some go to seed. If you collect and save seeds you'll have next year's batch ready to go once summer comes.

How to use it: The blossoms are mild but have a fresh flavor that brightens up a salad and will add flair to your next crudité platter.

BUDGET TIP: PLANTING SMALL IS PLANTING SMART

You can either spend an arm and a leg on your plants, or you can be smart. Plants are not furniture: they are alive and will get bigger. Plant sizes are one of the few places where you can save some money while creating your garden. You can buy fruit trees in 24-in. boxes, or you can buy a slightly smaller 15-gal. fruit tree for half the price. Many of the plants in your edible garden—nasturtiums, shiso, lettuces, borage, arugula, chamomile, and basil, among others—can be easily grown from seed. Plant small and stretch your budget at the same time you stretch your gardening muscles.

BANANAS
Musa ×*paradisiaca*

Tender perennial; large green leaves; thick, fleshy trunk; height varies from dwarf (7 ft.) to 30 ft.

If you live in a frost-free area of the country, plant a banana. Do it for those of us who can't. The gloriously long, thick, paddle-shaped leaves make the banana the definitive statement plant. Even if you don't have a tropical-style garden, a banana can fit in and create a special, full-stop moment. On an already over-the-top beautiful plant, the fruiting stalk is a striking ornamental feature—it looks like a prehistoric plant/bird hybrid. Who wouldn't want that stopping traffic in front of their house?

How to grow it: With such huge leaves and delicious, nutritious fruit, bananas are one of the heaviest feeders in the plant world. Compost is key to successful growing, as is extra nitrogen and potassium. If you happen to have chickens, use composted manure mixed with wood ash to top dress the bananas throughout the year. Bananas need consistently frost-free weather to develop a fruiting stalk. If there is a freeze, the rhizomes will survive and the leaves will return. Hardy in zones 9–11.

How to use it: A banana leaf works great as a wrapper to steam fish, or as a decorative liner on platter of hors d'oeuvres. Most people prefer to eat their bananas fresh but they are also served fried in the Caribbean as a sweet accompaniment to rice and beans. You can also try planting the varieties that produce the green, starchy plantain, which is savory, crispy, and delectable when fried.

OPPOSITE, TOP: Bachelor's buttons are cheerful, colorful, easy to grow, and love to play peek-a-boo through more permanent plantings. Throw out a handful of seeds and see where the flowers turn up. Photo by Ivette Soler

OPPOSITE, BOTTOM: Many edible grow easily from seed. This will save money and often give you the opportunity to find varieties that aren't readily available at nurseries. Photo by Ivette Soler

BASIL
Ocimum species

....

Tender annual; foliage ranges from red to purple to green; lavender flowers on spikes; summer bloom; 18 in. tall and wide; 75 days to maturity.

....

Basil deserves a special pride of place in the edible front yard. It is scrumptious, easy to grow, and as ornamental as any plant could hope to be. One of my favorites, *Ocimum basilicum* 'Siam Queen', has deep green leaves, purple bracts, and beautiful dusky flowers that resemble little bouquets. Its flavor is spicy with a hint of licorice, perfect for adventurous Asian cooking. Another tremendous basil is the purple-tinged 'African Blue'. It blooms early in the season but the flowering doesn't affect the flavor of the leaves, allowing you to let your basil flower and eat it too. The classic large, deep green leaves of 'Genovese' are just as useful for their visual impact in a garden as they are in an Italian kitchen. The columnar 'Pesto Perpetuo' has a surprising creamy variegation to its leaves and is a standout among other herbs and vegetables. The purple varieties, such as 'Purple Ruffles' and 'Red Rubin', are "team basil" all-stars of the edible front yard. Combine them with abandon and don't worry about planting too many. The spicy scent of basil perfuming your front yard on a warm afternoon is a heady delight.

How to grow it: Basil is a classic Mediterranean herb that loves heat and sharp drainage. It grows beautifully in raised beds, but you can plant it in the ground if you add compost and a little sandy grit to your soil. Flowering affects the flavor of most basil varieties, so it is important to keep the blooms pinched back. If you use basil as much as I do, that won't be a problem. Annual in all zones.

How to use it: Classic sweet basil brushes everything it touches with an unmistakable Mediterranean flavor: in salads, in sandwiches, as a flavoring for oil, and of course, tossed fresh into pasta or made into pesto. Use Thai and purple basil in wraps, vegetable dishes, and even teas. Experiment with the distinctive flavors of the different varieties—they are as tasty as they are lovely.

....

OPPOSITE, TOP: The always attractive 'African Blue' basil flowers early, but the maroon-kissed leaves don't turn bitter, making it as useful in the kitchen as it is in the garden. Photo by Ann Summa

OPPOSITE, BOTTOM: 'Red Rubin' basil runs with a tough crowd in my front yard. Photo by Ann Summa

BEANS
Phaseolus, Vicia, and *Vigna* species

....

*Annual; vining trifoliate leaves; color and size varies;
mid-summer bloom; 60–90 days to maturity.*

....

Edible pod beans—snap beans or string beans—have
truly come into their own as ornamental plants. They
can't be called plain old green beans anymore. Find
selections in a variety of colors like yellow, purple, white,
and even spotted and striped. Pole beans (*Phaseolus*),
which need the support of a trellis or a teepee structure,
provide a great opportunity to incorporate strong vertical
elements into the garden. The standout pole bean, in
terms of ornamental appeal, is the scarlet runner bean
(*P. coccineus*) which has profuse, beautiful red flowers
that hang in clusters; it is often planted just for its flowers alone. *P. vulgaris* 'Royal Burgundy' has glossy purple
pods that are incredibly attractive. Another wonderful
bean is the yard-long bean (*Vigna sinensis*), whose pods
are slender and sinewy (and very long); it is unusual, delicious, and adds tremendous interest to a planting. Fava
beans (*Vicia fava*) are also not to be overlooked; they
have white flowers with a black blotch in the center, and
only need minimal support.

How to grow it: Over-fertilizing beans can result in
too many leaves and a lack of bean pods; planting them
in amended beds is enough (legumes make their own
nitrogen, so their presence actually improves the soil).
Take the opportunity pole beans give you to grow up—
over arbors, on screens, up trellises—and add vertical
interest to your front yard. You will need to help your
beans onto their supports as they start to grow, and bird
netting will help keep the beans in your garden and out
of the grasp of your neighborhood's feathered hooligans.
Annual in all zones.

How to use it: Steamed or sautéed, in soups or salads,
even French fried: beans are a must for the kitchen and
the garden. You can also try tossing the edible leaves of
fava beans into a salad.

....

OPPOSITE: The blooms of scarlet runner beans satisfy vegetable
gardeners with an eye for color and drama. Photo by Ivette Soler

BEETS
Beta vulgaris

....

Herbaceous biennial grown as an annual; large, crinkly leaves (green, green with red veins, or bright red) and thick stalk attached to a round root; 1 ft. tall × 6 in. wide; 65 days to maturity.

....

In the ornamental front yard edible garden, *Beta vulgaris* 'Bull's Blood' stands high above other beets. The deeply hued leaves of this plant, and the magenta stems that burst out of the beetroot's ruddy shoulders, are undeniably glorious. The mighty, iron-rich beet grows best in cool weather, making it an asset for the spring garden: a leafy mound of crimson that brightly cuts through the green freshness of the season.

How to grow it: Plant beets as early in the season as you can work the soil. They grow best when temperatures are cool and the sun is bright. The best soil is light and loamy, without any amending other than compost. If you sow seeds, you can expect germination within a week to ten days. Keep a close eye on them, you'll have to thin the leaves so the beets can form sturdy, delicious roots.

How to use it: Be careful! Beets are bloody and weep a lot, so make sure to wear an apron when you handle them, even when harvesting. The leaf trimmings are great in micro-green salads. You can also sauté the leaves with fennel and onions for an earthy taste sensation. The beets themselves are a glory when roasted with salt and pepper. Or make ruby colored beet chips to wow your next dinner party: slice the beets extra thinly, toss them with olive oil, salt, pepper, and lemon zest, and roast them in a convection oven for an hour at 275 degrees.

BLUEBERRIES
Vaccinium species

....

Perennial shrub; green leaves; bell-shaped flowers turn from green to light blue in most varieties; spreading habit; average height of 3–4 ft.

....

Blueberries are very nice looking, yummy, anti-oxidant powerhouses. These shrubs are worthy of inclusion in a garden on the strength of the beautiful foliage alone, and they have a fantastic fall color that adds excitement to the end of the growing season. The flowers are charming little fairy bells, and the berries themselves are just as delightful. Blueberries are irresistible to children—plant a blueberry shrub or two and you will easily turn your children into fruit eaters and garden lovers.

How to grow it: Blueberries make excellent ornamental edibles, but watch out, they don't like hot summers and they need soil with an acid bite. These plants are best grown in temperate summer climates. If your zone fits the bill, plant away! If you live where summers are very warm, then try 'Bluetta' or 'Misty', which have low chill requirements. Blueberries need two different varieties within 100 ft. of each other to pollinate—the more the merrier. Hardy in zones 3–9.

How to use it: Desserts, smoothies, and cereal toppings aren't the only ways to enjoy the amazing blueberry. Take a walk on the savory side: make a vinaigrette with a blueberry reduction, or toss some into a crab salad. Blueberries are nicely balanced between salty and sweet, so they can go anywhere your heart desires.

....

OPPOSITE: Borage is a cottage garden favorite: a sturdy, tough-as-nails plant made up of dainty blue shooting stars. Photo by Ann Summa

BORAGE

Borago officinalis

....

Herbaceous annual; gray-green, rough, furry leaves; blue, pink, or white flowers; summer bloom; 24 in. tall × 18 in. wide; 70–80 days to maturity.

....

If, while strolling through a garden, you see little blue shooting stars exploding over a fountain of fuzzy leaves, you have stumbled upon borage. The luminous clusters of pinky-purple buds start off pendulous, then rear up and make themselves known with a burst of color. The edible grayish-green fuzzy leaves and stems of borage are a wonderful foil for darker foliage in the garden.

How to grow it: Borage doesn't need anything special. Sow the seeds (or plant from nursery starts) and the rest is simple. It is a prolific self-sower, but borage is so lovely that I have yet to find a place where it is not welcome. Enjoy the easy going nature of this pretty plant.

How to use it: All parts of the borage plant taste like cucumber. Pick the leaves young or they will become hairy and prickly (older leaves can be quick-sautéed and the prickliness will disappear). The flowers are fantastic in salads and sandwiches, and even better frozen in ice cubes and added to drinks. A Bloody Mary with borage ice is a foolproof crowd pleaser.

....

OPPOSITE: The magenta stems of ruby chard combined with a few 'Sungold' tomatoes create quite a sensation in this edible front yard. Photo by Ivette Soler

CHARD

Beta vulgaris var. *cicla*

....

Biennial grown as an annual; green or red leaves; stems and midribs in a wide variety of colors; 20 in. tall × 18 in. wide; 50–60 days to maturity.

....

Chard is a powerhouse both in the garden and the kitchen. With colorful stems and deeply veined leaves it's as beautiful as a plant gets—don't pass up adding one (or ten!) of the dynamic and delicious varieties to your garden. Ruby chard can singe your eye with its beauty, and rainbow chard is a color carnival. Chard is so good for you too: high in vitamins A, C, and K, as well as chock full of iron, potassium, and fiber. Chard also helps our bones hold onto calcium, and it contains magnesium, which works in concert with calcium to help keep us calm and relaxed.

How to grow it: Chard wants fertile, well-drained soil. Like most leafy vegetables, it appreciates nitrogen, so water with half-strength fish emulsion or worm tea throughout the season. Harvest by cutting the individual leaves—it will rejuvenate itself so you can enjoy its bounty all season long. Reliably annual in all zones, it can overwinter in zones 9–10.

How to use it: When harvested very young, chard is delicious in a mixed greens salad. When mature, sauté it or add it to soups. Don't forget the delicious stems, which you can caramelize by quickly roasting.

CITRUS
Citrus species

Evergreen trees; green leaves with white fragrant flowers; bloom time varies, mostly mid- to late spring; 12–30 ft. tall × 12–25 ft. wide.

Lemons, limes, oranges, clementines, kumquats—that's just the tip of the iceberg when it comes to citrus varieties available to the home gardener. If you live in a climate that allows for the easy growing of citrus, do it. If you have to trick your zone a little by planting citrus trees against a south-facing wall, try it. Picking home-grown organic lemons from your front yard rather than paying 99 cents per lemon every time you need one makes good economic sense. You can also explore the range of citrus not always available in markets, such as citrons, pumelos, tangelos, blood oranges, and more. Not only will you have a wonderful evergreen tree in your front yard, you will have the sensual and alluring fragrance of the citrus flowers. Plant more than one of the dwarf varieties and add an astringent kick to your garden and your kitchen.

How to grow it: Citrus trees need warm, temperate climates to thrive. You can create a comfortable microclimate by placing your tree against a south-facing wall and giving it reflected heat from sidewalks or even your neighbor's house. Citrus trees are heavy feeders, so amend the planting area with plenty of compost. After planting a citrus tree top dress with worm compost for an added punch of extra nitrogen. Hardy to zone 9.

How to use it: The ways to employ citrus in the kitchen are endless: the juice can be used in dressings, marinades, or drinks (mojitos, anyone?), and just one squirt adds an acidic dimension to your cooking. Zest the skins of citrus fruits to get the flavor into your food without the acid, or candy the skins and use them to decorate cakes and cookies. The fragrance of lemons, limes, and grapefruits has an energizing aromatherapeutic value. Make uplifting sachets for your drawers by simply drying thin slices of citrus in a convection oven or dehydrator until free of moisture, and wrapping them in a muslin bundle.

CORN
Zea mays

Annual; large, wavy leaves, usually green; ears mainly white or yellow, occasionally blue, red, or bicolored; 6–8 ft. tall; 80–120 days to maturity.

Vertical elements are very important features within a landscape of mounding shrubs, and corn is just about as vertical as a plant can get. Corn grows rapidly so you could even make a temporary screen—a corn fence—in the summer. You can also take a page from the Native Americans and grow corn as a trellis for beans. Play with the beautiful varieties: *Zea mays* 'Japonica Striped' has bicolored leaves, *Z. mays* 'Rainbow Inca' has gorgeous ears. But even plain old green corn's long leaves arch and wave ornamentally in the slightest breeze.

How to grow it: Corn is an hermaphrodite: each plant has both male flowers (the tassel) and female flowers (silks from the ear). Grow corn in close proximity to each other (in rows or circles) so neighbors can help pollinate each other. Once the silks and tassels develop, you can gently shake your corn to encourage the pollen grains from the tassels to hit their silky targets. Corn loves nitrogen, so plant it in well-composted soil and give it an extra dose of organic fertilizer when planting. Water it with fish emulsion or worm tea once a week and try to keep the ears dry once they develop. The pollen is in the tassels so if the tassels are wet when pollination should be occurring, all you'll get is cob. Annual in all zones.

How to use it: There are so many ways to enjoy corn, but sweet summer corn is best enjoyed on the cob, when grilled over an open fire. Basta.

OPPOSITE, TOP LEFT: A small ear of corn early in the season is a mop-top of tassels. Here it compares hairdos with a mophead hydrangea. Photo by Ann Summa

OPPOSITE, TOP RIGHT Japanese eggplant, with its burnished purple, lanky stems, has a bit of a witchy vibe. Photo by Ann Summa

OPPOSITE, BOTTOM: Lemons dangle over a recycled wood and corrugated metal fence. Photo by Ann Summa

CUTTING CELERY
Apium graveolens var. *secalinum*

Perennial often grown as an annual; green foliage; 12–18 in. tall × 9–12 in. wide; 85 days to maturity.

Cutting celery doesn't form into the traditional bunch of stalks, instead, it is a loose collection of smaller stalks and flat, quarter-sized, mid- to deep green leaves. It gives you all the flavor of celery, even if you live in a climate where bunching celery is hard to grow. The leaves resemble parsley, but stay greener in hot climates. If you let it flower, it will seed itself around and come up in surprising places.

How to grow it: Plant cutting celery in good, rich soil, in a sunny position (unless you live in a hot zone, where you'll want to give it a little protection). Harvest often to encourage renewed growth of tasty leaves and to keep it from reaching gargantuan proportions. Perennial in zones 8–10, annual elsewhere.

How to use it: Cutting celery is great in soups, braises, salads, and mixed with parsley for an extra zip in garnishes.

EGGPLANT
Solanum melongena

Tender perennial often grown as an annual; light to dark green foliage with purple midveins; lavender or purple flowers; white, purple, or striped vegetables; rangy, open habit; summer bloom; up to 2 1/2 ft. tall × 1–2 ft. wide; 60–80 days to maturity.

There is something alluring about the burnished stems, elongated leaves, and purple, lacquered fruit of this slightly spooky member of the nightshade family. With so many lovely varieties to choose from, you can easily put on a fashion show of different eggplant models in your front yard. The best of the best are the Italian 'Rosa Bianca', which is striped lavender and ivory; the garden classic 'Black Beauty', with its enormous and cylindrical dusky fruit; and the adorable white 'Easter Egg', which looks like hard-boiled eggs hanging sweetly from a mini-tree.

How to grow it: Eggplant is a heavy feeder, but be careful not to overdo the nitrogen. Side dress your eggplant with bone meal to help the formation of those big luscious globes. Eggplant loves heat; give it a sunny spot where it can soak up the rays.

How to use it: Eggplant is great grilled or baked. It's also delicious sautéed or fried but it absorbs lots of oil when cooking, so watch how much you add.

FENNEL
Foeniculum vulgare

Perennial often grown as an annual; green or bronze foliage; yellow umbelliferous flowers; bulbs early summer, blooms mid-summer; up to 3 ft. tall × 1–2 ft. wide; 85–100 days to maturity.

The tall, wispy, feathery fronds of this magical edible are a wondrous sight. When fennel sways in the breeze, its elegance rivals any grass. And every part—bulb, leaves, seeds, and umbelliferous flowers—is scrumptious too. Two kinds of fennel are usually grown: bulbing or Florence (called *finocchio* in Italy) fennel, and bronze fennel (*Foeniculum vulgare* 'Purpureum'). Both types have edible seeds and leaves though only Florence fennel will produce the vegetable bulb. Bronze fennel is particularly ornamental—the incredible smokey haze of its fine-textured leaves creates a moody foil for other colors in the garden.

How to grow it: Fennel likes loose, rich soil. Place it in a little shade in hotter climates to discourage bolting. To keep bulbing fennel tender, start mounding mulch around the bulb when it swells. Cut off any blooming stalks to send more energy to the bulb until you are ready to harvest.

How to use it: The leaves and seeds (one of the central ingredients in Italian sausage) of both types of fennel display a subtle anise flavor. The tender stalks of bulbing fennel make a delicious substitute for celery in almost all dishes—even in a Bloody Mary.

OPPOSITE: Sporting dark and fluffy foxtail-like fronds that reach for its neighbor to stroke and tickle, bronze fennel is a favorite of any gardener who loves color and texture. Photo by Ann Summa

FIG
Ficus carica

....

Deciduous tree; big, green-lobed leaves; green or purple fruit; 10–30 ft. tall.

....

Figs have been famous ever since biblical times when their leaves were draped over the bodies of the newly shy Adam and Eve. But if Eve had tasted the fruit of the fig tree first, she might never have been tempted to bite the apple. Luscious, sweet, and syrupy, figs are thrilling on the tongue. And they're just as satisfying as garden plants: those legendary thick, deeply lobed, embossed-veined leaves are a masterpiece. Surprisingly, the fig itself isn't technically a fruit—we actually eat the bloom, which is hidden inside a special structure (the fig) that encloses the flower and the reproductive parts of the flower.

How to grow it: Figs love as much sun as they can get and less-than-rich soil. Don't over-fertilize with the intention of doing your tree a favor—you might end up with fewer figs. Fig trees are fast-growing and flexible enough to be easily espaliered against walls (planting a fig against a south-facing wall is a good way to get these trees into gardens in colder zones). Hardy to zone 7.

How to use it: Eat figs fresh or drizzled with honey—add a little goat cheese and you have a tasty appetizer. Make fig jam or preserves to experience a taste of this summer delight all year long.

GRAPES
Vitis species

....

Perennial woody vine needing strong support; green or purple leaves; spring bloom; size varies.

....

Grapes are beautiful, delicious, and versatile, though this is not the vine for the faint hearted—be prepared to put some work into their success. But if you choose the right variety and have the patience to make it work, you can have a great crop of fruit as well as a bold statement in your front yard. I adore purple-leaved *Vitis vinifera* 'Purpurea' because of the splendid color it adds to the garden.

How to grow it: Grapes need fertile soil so compost the planting area well. Grow them on a sturdy structure that will allow you easy access to the canes for a hard pruning every year. The canes need air to circulate around them for good fruit production, so keeping the vine well thinned is essential. You'll have to learn a few specific techniques, such as how to prune for maximum fruit set, but once you know your stuff you will have a fantastic addition to your garden. Bird netting helps you keep your grapes rather than donating them to the ravenous flock on the block. Hardy in zones 3–9.

How to use it: Grapes are the go-to fruit for jams, jellies, homemade wine, and vinegars. Don't forget about the leaves which can be blanched and stuffed to make tasty *dolmas*.

....

OPPOSITE: These red-leaved grapes are grown on a sturdy side fence, hiding their bounty among the mottled, late-season foliage. Photo by Ann Summa

JERUSALEM ARTICHOKE
Helianthus tuberosus

Perennial grown as an annual; green leaves, yellow flowers; upright flower can get up to 10 ft. tall × 2–4 ft. wide; summer bloom; 100 days to maturity.

Jerusalem artichoke (also called sunchoke) is a type of sunflower and is unrelated to the artichoke—its name derives from the artichoke-meets-potato flavor of the root. It looks like a giant version of a little kid's drawing with its cheerful, yellow, daisy-like flowers and simple green leaves,. These sunflowers are the very definition of a prairie summer and they do a fantastic job attracting bees, which improves the quality of all the edibles in your garden. Like other sunflowers, kids love Jerusalem artichokes; let your children be in charge of these easy-to-grow plants and give them a little push into the world of gardening.

How to grow it: In some parts of the United States, the Jerusalem artichoke is considered weedy. But when harvested at the end of the growing season, and its delicious roots consumed, the weed potential is minimal. Loosen up your garden soil before planting to encourage large tuber formation. Be careful not to fertilize too much: the goal is big roots not lots of leaves. Hardy in zones 5–10.

How to use it: Jerusalem artichokes are perfect in soups, stews, gratins, and when pickled. Raw, they taste similar to water chestnuts.

OPPOSITE, TOP: A young lemongrass plant proudly takes center stage in a raised hellstrip bed. Harvest often and enjoy its unique flavor in soups and sauces. Photo by Ivette Soler

OPPOSITE, BOTTOM: Lacinato kale is the darling of the culinary world, and gardeners love its rugged good looks and whimsical form. Photo by Juree Sondker

KALE
Brassica oleracea var. *acephala*

Biennial grown as an annual; color deep green to purple to red; habit varies from almost head-forming to a loose arrangement of leaves; 18–24 in. tall, width varies; 65–75 days to maturity.

Kale is gorgeous, delicious, and packs a nutritious wallop: it's a must for an edible garden. All kales are great but for the ornamental edible front yard, lacinato kale (also called cavolo nero) is the hands-down best choice. It has unusual, dark green (almost black) leaves that are slender, wrinkled, and curl and twist in interesting ways; it also has more phytonutrients than other varieties. 'Red Russian' kale runs a close second: its deeply cut leaves in shades of red or purple make a frilly, ladylike statement in the spring garden. These beautiful plants are packed full of flavor, with a unique balance of savory and bitter that sings on the palate.

How to grow it: Like all brassicas, kale likes cool weather. It will bolt when things warm up too much and the leaves will become unpleasantly bitter. In hot zones, try growing kale in the fall or winter. If you live in a temperate zone you can grow this easy plant throughout the season, but when temperatures soar, a little shade cloth to protect it from the hottest sun will help keep it growing well into fall. Plant in fertile soil and feed with fish emulsion or compost tea regularly; this heavy feeder needs a lot of nitrogen to make plenty of dark green leaves. Annual in all zones.

How to use it: Lacinato kale is a vegetable superstar and the darling of fine food circles. Cook it in soups, sautés, and pastas, or eat it raw in salads—you are limited only by your imagination. Its toothsome, hearty texture stands up to long cooking without becoming stringy or mushy. A fresh serving of homegrown kale will make a convert out of those who have turned up their noses in the past.

LEMONGRASS

Cymbopogon citratus

....

Tender perennial; green, grassy leaves; fountain-shaped; fall bloom; 3–5 ft. tall × 3 ft. wide.

....

Lemongrass is beautiful, versatile, and adds a delicious, specific flavor to food. Its big, generous, grassy shape is unusual in an edible garden, and that dynamic texture is very welcome. It grows to approximately 3 ft. tall (bigger in hot, humid areas) and has a graceful, almost ethereal quality. The slender leaves and arching form contrast well with other plants in the edible front yard.

How to grow it: Lemongrass used to be hard to come by, but thanks to the popularity of Asian foods, it can be found in starts at most local nurseries. It adapts to a variety of soils: grow it lean and you'll have a tidy little mound, grow it in amended soil in your raised beds and you'll have a luxurious monster of tasty beauty. At the end of the growing season, divide it up and share your bounty with friends—pot up a few stalks to bring inside as next year's plants. Those in warm climates can have lemongrass in their gardens all year long. Perennial in zones 9–11, annual elsewhere.

How to use it: Harvest lemongrass by cutting off stalks at the root. Use it in teas, soups, and marinades. Thinly slivered slices of lemongrass are excellent in stirfries.

....

OPPOSITE: Beautiful, ruby-red looseleaf lettuce is a perfect edging for a path, and you can nibble on the trimmings. Photo by Ann Summa

LETTUCE

Lactuca sativa

....

Annual; green, red, or speckled color; heading or looseleaf, upright habit; size varies but usually 6–8 in. tall and wide; 45–55 days to maturity

....

Lettuces are an automatic given—how can you have an edible garden and not plant such visually appealing plants? Lettuces are available in a wide array of colors (some are even speckled), shapes, and sizes; the leaves range from smooth and elongated to crinkled and highly textured. Planting a swath of lettuces is a wonderful way to create a visual rest in an active garden. Their small size also makes them wonderful plants for the front of the border. They help to create a finished look that gives the edible garden a more traditionally ornamental feel.

How to grow it: Lettuce is among the easiest edibles to grow from seed. Prepare your planting area with a generous amount of compost, then sprinkle your seeds where you want them. As they sprout and grow, thin your lettuces by clipping the tiny leaves with scissors (manicure scissors work perfectly). This helps promote air circulation and avoid the dreaded damping off, a fungal condition that causes seedlings to wilt and die. Save the thinnings for micro-green salads. Harvest heading lettuces before the center begins to elongate or the leaves will be bitter. For looseleaf lettuces, just cut the leaves as you need them and the lettuce will rejuvenate from the stem. Lettuce grows best in cool temperatures (55–78 degrees) but some varieties, such as 'Black-Seeded Simpson', grow well in hot zones.

How to use it: The fresh leaves of lettuces are at the heart of spring and early summer salads, and can also be used as a substitute for sandwich bread, pitas, or tortillas in roll-ups. Don't stop there: have you ever had lettuce soup? It's an excellent way to use parts of the plant, like the ribs or tough leaves, that would normally go to waste.

🌿 a lettuce lawn 🌿

Who needs sod? Even the word *sod* sounds bad, like something you don't want in front of your house. I propose something entirely different—a crisp green (or red or speckled) carpet of one of our freshest, yummiest edibles. It is easy and inexpensive to create, and can be maintained with less effort than goes into a regular lawn. If you live in a hotter climate, site your lettuce lawn in a dappled area rather than in the bright hot sun. Regular cutting (and eating) will help keep your lettuce from bolting. If you seed, weed, and eat at regular intervals, you should be able to maintain your lettuce lawn all summer long.

Materials

- Enough lettuce starts to cover 1/4 of the area
- Several packets of lettuce seeds
- Water

Steps

1. Select or create a sod-free area for your lettuce lawn and lightly dig in a generous amount of compost.

2. Plant your baby lettuces in an evenly spaced manner. They will look like hair plugs, but this is only the beginning: these lettuces will kickstart your lawn.

3. Take your packets and broadcast the lettuce seeds between the lettuce plants. You can sow these seeds fairly thickly because you will be harvesting continually as they grow.

4. Water in the seeds. You don't need to cover them with soil—the water will set the tiny seeds far enough in the ground for germination. Be sure to keep the lettuce lawn moist while the seeds are germinating.

Note:

Choose your favorite kind (or kinds) of non-heading lettuce. These are known as cut-and-come-again because new leaves will refresh the old ones as you harvest them. You won't need to harvest an entire head and leave a hole.

MARJORAM
Origanum marjorana

Perennial herb; green with green elongated bracts; tiny white flowers; early to mid-summer bloom; 2 1/2 ft. tall and wide.

This bushy perennial is often overlooked, both as an herb in the kitchen and as a valuable player in the garden. Marjoram is closely related to oregano, but has a sweeter, more complex taste. Don't plant oregano alone thinking that you have both bases covered—there's room for both of these wonderful herbs in the ornamental front yard edible garden. Marjoram is a perfect filler for small gaps among perennials and its dainty white flowers tucked into elongated bracts are among the most powerful attractors of bees I've ever seen.

How to grow it: A true Mediterranean herb, this plant likes it rough and tough. It grows better in soil that is lean, almost rocky, rather than amended. Perennial in zones 8–10, annual elsewhere.

How to use it: The unique flavor of marjoram really sings when used fresh in salads that have a meat component—or whenever you want to round out a dish with its sweet, herbal flavor. To preserve its brightness, add marjoram at the end of the cooking process. For a real treat, take it into the bath with you. The clean, fresh scent will surround you with warm, fragrant herbal pleasure.

OPPOSITE: Never plant mint directly in the ground. This window box makes a nice (contained) home for variegated pineapple mint, ruby chard, edible pansies, and thyme. Photo by Ann Summa. Garden of Theresa Loe

MINT
Mentha species

....

Perennial herb; green, variegated, or bronze-tinged foliage; shrubby and spreading habit; 6–18 in. tall.

....

Alert: mint is infamously invasive. Besides spreading via underground runners, the stems will root if any leaf node touches the ground. Whew! Now that that stern warning is out of the way, let me say that you should definitely include mint in your edible garden. Choose from many great varieties in different colors with subtle variations in taste. Cooking with freshly plucked mint is a completely different experience than making do with what you can get at markets—and it is so easy to grow.

How to grow it: Even though it wants to be a groundcover, mint should never be planted directly into the ground—it will become a rampant bully in no time. Always contain your mint in pots, hanging baskets, or a raised bed devoted to mint and mint alone. Mint grows effortlessly in sun, shade, and even drought. In fact, you would have to severely interfere to get it not to grow. Perennial in zones 5–11, annual elsewhere.

How to use it: My favorite mint for cooking is spearmint, and I use peppermint in hot and cold drinks. Mint is essential when cooking Asian food; its zingy freshness brightens every dish. It is especially refreshing when added to cold drinks like lemonade, iced tea, or punches. Mint tea is said to aid digestion, so treat yourself to a cup brewed with fresh leaves after an evening of overindulgence.

MUSTARD GREENS
Brassica juncea

....

Cool-season annual; greenish red foliage, large savoyed (crinkled) leaves; 1–2 ft. tall and wide; 60–80 days to maturity.

....

Two kinds of mustard greens truly deserve the front and center treatment. The first is 'Red Giant' mustard (also known as spinach mustard), a loosely headed cluster of large crinkled leaves with a deep maroon coloration that is set off by creamy white midribs and veins. It is an ideal front-of-the-border plant that easily integrates into an ornamental planting of perennials and shrubs. The other noteworthy mustard is 'Red Coral' (or 'Red Streak') Japanese mizuna; the delicate, incised leaves are a welcome opportunity to experiment with textural combinations. The deep colors of these mustards are a welcome addition to the paler, fresher colors of spring. Try planting them with red violas for a monochromatic punch.

How to grow it: Mustard seeds germinate readily and the plant grows rapidly; as long as the soil has been amended and kept moist, you should have success. One thing to watch out for is the horror of the brassicas—the evil cabbage worm. Don't think that nefarious schemes aren't being hatched if you see small white butterflies flitting around your mustards. They are indeed, in the form of tiny green worms that will devour the delicious leaves. If you see the butterflies, start inspecting your mustards and wash off the undersides with a strong jet of water every few days for two weeks; you should be able to wash away any eggs and young worms. You can also underplant mustards with nasturtiums. Besides forming an attractive visual association, the nasturtiums will act as a trap crop inviting the worms to gorge on their mild leaves rather than the tangy, hot foliage of mustard.

How to use it: Make sure to harvest mustard greens before they bloom and become bitter. Enjoy mustard as you would spinach: in salads when young and sautéed when mature. These plants have a horseradish-like bite, so use accordingly. Add some zip to your pesto by sneaking a few leaves of red mustard into the mix—this will certainly wake up your pasta.

NASTURTIUMS
Tropaeolum majus

....

Annual; green, lilypad-shaped leaves; orange or yellow flowers; groundcover, climbing, or mounding habit; spring to summer bloom; size varies.

....

Is it an herb? A vegetable? An edible flower? The nasturtium is all of these things. This pretty flowering annual is synonymous with cottage garden charm. The cheerful colors and shapes of this plant delight the eye as well as the palate. Who can resist those surprising whirligig blooms? If you like it hot, you'll love the strident "look at me" orange of the classic nasturtium flower. And if not, choose from the practically endless range of flower colors, from the softest yellow to peachy pink, clear red, or deepest maroon. The lilypad-shaped leaves are no slouches, either. Some are variegated, some are fresh grassy green, and a few varieties are tinged with a dark, steely blue-green.

How to grow it: High-spirited nasturtiums are embarrassingly easy to grow. Plant the seeds in your regular garden soil (too rich and you'll get an overabundance of leaves and few flowers)—in five days you'll have germination, within a few weeks you'll have little plants, and blooms will quickly follow. Don't bother buying starter plants; the fast-growing seeds come in a wider choice of colors.

How to use it: All parts of a nasturtium are edible. The colorful, crunchy, peppery flowers are delectable for salads and garnishes. The leaves are a great substitute for watercress. The seeds can be pickled and used the way you'd use capers—they can even be dried and used as a pepper substitute. Plant nasturtiums throughout your edible garden as a trap crop for aphids.

....

OPPOSITE: This nasturtium has decided to climb a ladder to see what's on the other side. The exuberance of the lilypad leaves and whirligig flowers is unstoppable. Photo by Ivette Soler

NEXT PAGE: A leek flower stands tall and proud. Photo by Ann Summa

ONIONS, GARLIC, CHIVES, AND LEEKS
Allium species

Biennials and perennials; strappy green foliage; white or pinky-purple blossoms; size and shape varies (chives are smaller and grow in grassy clumps; garlic, onions, and leeks have a few leaves per bulb); summer bloom; 90–140 days to maturity.

All alliums—onions, garlic, chives, and leeks—can be used to fill in space at the base of larger, leggier plants. Some, like the mighty leek, are incredibly ornamental, with round globes perched atop thin yet sturdy stems. Onions are a fabulous addition to an edible garden with an ornamental focus. The strappy leaves are a great stand-in for grasses (those textural superstars of the ornamental garden) and the blossoms are enchanting little orbs of tastiness.

How to grow it: Plant onions in loose, friable soil, setting them in deeper than they sit in their nursery pots. Make certain the drainage is good—raised beds are perfect for planting onions. Should they start to push themselves out of the soil, cover their shoulders with a mulch of compost. Harvest when they reach the desired size—usually when 1/4 to 1/2 of the green tops have fallen over. Plant long day onions if you live in northern states, and short day onions if you live in the South.

How to use it: Alliums are essential in the kitchen. Onions, along with celery and peppers, make up a classic *mirepoix*, the base for most traditional French savory cooking. And all parts of these amazing plants are edible: toss chive flowers in a salad or garlic blossoms in a stirfry for a piquant treat.

ORACH
Atriplex hortensis

Annual; green, red, or purple foliage; erect habit; harvest before early summer bloom; up to 2 ft. tall × 1.5 ft. wide; 45–60 days to maturity (use young leaves).

This leafy vegetable is an ancient edible, but for some reason it is almost never found in markets—traditional or farmers. It's up to us home gardeners to grow and enjoy this beautiful green. Actually, "green" might be the wrong word to use—the reason I grew orach in the first place was for the red color of the arrowhead-shaped leaves. The stems and bracts of the flowers are the same dusky color, making it matchy-matchy, but in a good way.

How to grow it: Find seeds for this attractive spinach substitute in seed catalogs and sow the minute frost danger has passed. Sow in fertile soil, well amended with compost and a booster of well-rotted chicken manure if you have it. Orach doesn't tolerate heat, so give it the organic fertilizer and water it needs to grow fast. It doesn't transplant well, which is probably why starts aren't available in nurseries. Annual in all zones.

How to use it: Enjoy versatile orach fresh in salads, sautéed, or in stews.

OREGANO
Origanum vulgare

Perennial herb; green to greenish gray to chartreuse foliage; white, pink, or purple flowers; sprawling groundcover; summer to fall bloom; 6–12 in. tall.

Oregano is no stranger to the ornamental garden. When it flowers, the profuse blossoming clusters will fill the garden with bees. While all oregano is worthy of a spot in the front yard, my all-time favorite is the spectacular golden oregano (*Origanum vulgare* 'Aureum')—the gilt color is simply out of this world. Its small size makes it a wonderful front-of-border plant or an important component in a colorful herbal carpet. Golden oregano grabs the eye and won't let go—especially when combined with reds and purples.

How to grow it: Like other Mediterranean herbs, oregano shouldn't be pampered. Grow it in full sun in unamended soil and the plants will have a nice flavor. Keep oregano on the dry side to avoid root rot. Hardy in zones 5–11.

How to use it: Pizza or spaghetti sauce without oregano? Never. Oregano's sharp, warm, almost resinous flavor is unmistakable. Use in Italian, Greek, and Mexican dishes. The flavor is often improved when dried—an hour or two in an oven set on low will give you that strength you need for bolder cooking applications.

PADDLE CACTUS
Opuntia ficus-indica

Perennial; green fleshy paddles; yellow blooms emerge from deep pink buds; summer bloom; up to 10 ft. tall and wide.

What is the paddle cactus doing on this list? Is this madness? No, it isn't—*Opuntia ficus-indica* is a delicious edible enjoyed by Latino cultures and served in some of the finest restaurants. In the garden, paddle cactus (also called prickly pear) is an unexpected combination of the statuesque and the whimsical. When young, the paddle "ears" can't help but remind one of Mickey Mouse, but as it gets bigger it becomes a true statement plant. The big, yellow, almost tropical flowers form a surprisingly lush contrast to the spare, succulent texture of the paddles. This impressive plant is easily grown in Mediterranean climates—it flourishes in the west and southwest—but those who live in colder zones should give it a chance too. Once planted, enjoyed, harvested, and tasted, I predict the cultivation of paddle cactus will spread north.

How to grow it: Paddle cactus thrives naturally in rocky soils, but when growing for ornamental and edible purposes, plant it in amended soil—you'll get faster growth and thicker, more flavorful paddles. Hardy in zones 8–10.

How to use it: This melting pot country provides us the opportunity to sample the best of so many other cultures. The (skinned) interior of the young stems is a delicious Mexican staple called *nopales*. The flavor is distinctive but mild, somewhere between a green bean, sweet pepper, and asparagus, with a little okra thrown in. Nopales are delicious in frittatas, omelettes, sandwiches, soups, and stews. Use the paddle as you would a bell pepper, but be certain to skin its spiny outer layer first. The red fruit can be skinned, roasted, and then transformed into candies, jellies, and drinks. This exotic plant expands our garden palette and our culinary palate at the same time.

PARSLEY
Petroselinum crispum

Biennial herb; green leaves, wavy and curly or flat and serrated; yellow unbelliferous blooms; 18 in. tall and wide; 80–100 days to maturity.

The pleasant, fresh, crayola green color of parsley is always welcome in the garden, and its size allows it to be tucked here and there among other edibles and ornamentals. The flowers are little yellow umbrellas that attract bees like nobody's business. In my garden, I find room for both flat Italian parsley (*Petroselinum crispum* var. *neapolitanum*) and traditional curly parsley (*P. crispum*). The flat parsley is indispensable in the kitchen and curly parsley is delightful in the garden. Why choose? Plant both and there will always be a burst of freshness for your eye and on your tongue.

How to grow it: Parsley seeds are slow to germinate. Since the started plants are readily available at most nurseries, save yourself some time (unless you need to practice patience) and buy the starts. Plant in fertile, well-amended soil. Like most crops grown for their leaves, parsley loves nitrogen, so feel free to add some well-rotted chicken manure to your soil. Your plants will be green, lush, and tasty. If you live in a hot climate, site your parsley in dappled shade—it will appreciate the cooler conditions. Parsley starts blooming with heat and will bolt in the spring if it gets too warm.

How to use it: If the color green had a taste, it would be the fresh flavor of parsley. Sprinkle it on top of pasta and meats, or use the leaves whole in salads and on sandwiches. Though its mildness makes it disappear when cooked, a popular use is a quick sauté with garlic and butter—add to pasta with freshly cracked pepper for a taste of heaven. Parsley is a stealth bomb of nutrition loaded with iron, beta carotene, calcium, and B vitamins. Keep adding more parsley to your front yard edible garden and more of it will find a way into your diet.

OPPOSITE, TOP: It may be a stretch, but try growing the edible succulent *Opuntia ficus-indica* in your front yard. Its cartoon-like paddles and bright flowers make it a true standout. Photo by Ivette Soler

OPPOSITE, BOTTOM: A swath of Italian parsley conceals a small bench tucked into a planting of lavender and grasses. Photo by Ivette Soler

PASSIONFLOWER
Passiflora species

....

Perennial vine; green trifoliate leaves with clear blue or purple flowers that have prominent stamens; blooms year-round in temperate climates; size varies.

....

This glorious vine thrives in warm temperatures, but it is worth pushing it a zone or two to get one growing in your garden! The fruiting varieties of *Passiflora* are an almost perfect garden plant—beautiful, edible, a powerful hummingbird and bee attractant, and a food source for butterflies. The mid-green, tri-lobed leaves create a smooth, uninterrupted background for the startling flowers. The visual impact of these flowers cannot be overstated: each is a circle of clear, lavender petals surrounding a disc of neon purple stamens, with a red, attenuated pistil in the center. And hundreds of these wonders grow on one vine. A glory to behold.

How to grow it: *Passiflora edulis* is most cultivated variety for fruit, but *P. incarnata* is hardier and can be successfully grown even in zones prone to frost. If you plant it in full sun, or on a fence (the fence will hold and radiate heat, giving your vine an extra blanket of warmth), you should be able to get fruit set within a few years. The wait is certainly worth it. Passionflowers are heavy feeders, so top dress with compost frequently. Hardy in zones 8–10 (but try it elsewhere!)

How to use it: Eat passionfruit fresh, or add the pulp to smoothies and blended juices. It also makes an incredible sorbet.

....

OPPOSITE, TOP: The blossoms of the passionflower are small works of art, and the fruit that follows is a taste of the tropics. This is a wonderful screening vine for those in the right climate. Photo by Ivette Soler

OPPOSITE, BOTTOM LEFT: A young rhubarb is biding its time, getting ready to spread out in this front yard in the Silverlake district of Los Angeles. Photo by Ann Summa

OPPOSITE, BOTTOM RIGHT: Peppers come in enough colors, shapes, and flavors to suit any edible gardener. Dark green 'Ancho San Luis' pepper turns deep red as it ages and dries. Photo by Ann Summa

PEPPERS
Capsicum annuum

....

Perennial grown as an annual; green leaves; white flowers; fruits of various colors; mainly open, bushy habit; summer bloom; 65–80 days to maturity.

....

Sweet, hot, floral, piquant—there is truly a pepper for everybody. Peppers have endless ornamental applications; the colorful variety of the fruit makes them knockouts in the late summer edible garden. If you are mad for heat (for the eye as well as the palate), then plant my favorites—habaneros and Scotch bonnets. They hang innocently on the plant, like little folded lanterns decorating a mini tree, but are dangerously, mouth-searingly hot. Or try the long, thin, bright red cayenne, which looks fantastic next to eggplants. If you eschew the heat, play with sweet or banana peppers in colors ranging from orange and red to brown and purple; try varieties like 'Purple Beauty' or 'Lilac Hybrid'. Whichever type of pepper you decide to plant, it's hard to go wrong with these delicious beauties.

How to grow it: Peppers are an easy vegetable to grow, especially in hot climates. If you live in a temperate zone, start your seeds indoors and set them out when it's nice and warm—well after the last frost date. Plant in direct sunlight and be ready to protect with a cover should a random cold event threaten.

How to use it: Eat fresh bell peppers in salads and sandwiches for a satisfying crunch and flavor explosion. Hot peppers are most often used in salsas, but can add a level of zip to all of your savory dishes if used with a light touch. Experiment! Once you go hot, it's hard to cook without that special type of fire.

PLUM
Prunus domestica

....

Deciduous tree; green to purple foliage; white to pink flowers; small to medium sized trees with open crown; spring bloom; 12–15 ft. tall × 8–10 ft. wide.

....

Plum trees are lovely in blossom, in leaf, and especially in fruit when the heavy orbs hang from delicate branches. They aren't too big so they make a great understory tree to mediate between the large street trees and the lower levels of the garden. Some fruit is deep purple with a frosty bloom on the skin, others are red or yellow—all have a mouthwatering, sweet-tart flavor when ripe. Imagine how wonderful it will feel to pick the first plum of summer and eat it right under the tree in your front yard.

How to grow it: Keep in mind that many fruiting trees will need pollinators, which means planting more than one tree. Plum trees don't take well to the space-saving espalier technique so, unless you have the desire and sufficient space to create a mini-orchard, I suggest you choose a self-pollinating variety from one of the many wonderful choices. Supply generously amended soil and keep the tree evenly watered (not too wet, not too dry) for the best results. Hardy in zones 4–10.

How to use it: Eat plums fresh, or dry them to concentrate the sugars and turn plums into prunes. Both fresh and dried are staples in desserts.

RHUBARB
Rheum rhaponticum

....

Perennial often grown as an annual; green, heavily savoyed foliage; large ruby red stalks; tiny flowers emerge from tightly packed buds; late spring to early summer bloom; 3 ft. tall × 4 ft. wide.

....

Another name for rhubarb is "pie plant" because it is so commonly used for that purpose, but that moniker is much too folksy for this majestic plant. Rhubarb's thick, fleshy, bat wing leaves and crimson stalks demand attention. Its royal presence is equally matched by a royal temperament; it is fussy about temperature, only growing well in cooler parts of the country. If you are lucky enough to have this plant thrive in your garden, by all means grow it. It has the ornamental impact of that other architectural edible, the artichoke, with equally impressive leaves. Those who live in warm climates don't have to totally despair; you can grow rhubarb as an annual. It will be smaller than those gigantic ones grown as perennials, but a little rhubarb is better than no rhubarb at all.

How to grow it: Rhubarb is a heavy feeder—just one look at those leaves will tell you that. Mulching the plant in the winter with well-composted manure will set you up for a great harvest come spring. Pick the stems as you need them instead of harvesting the entire plant. When the weather gets too warm the taste will become bitter so let your rhubarb bloom and enjoy the dramatic flower. Hardy in zones 2–8.

How to use it: The leaves of rhubarb are decidedly not edible—in other words, poisonous—so keep them out of your kitchen. Cook the beautiful stalks and use them in pies, jams, and compotes. The classic pairing of rhubarb and strawberries strikes a magnificent culinary chord.

ROSE
Rosa species

Perennial; green alternate compound leaves, huge array of flower colors; size and habit varies with species; blooms in waves through spring and summer.

Though roses sometimes get a bad rap for being too frou frou, they are a fantastic choice for the front yard edible gardener with an eye on the ornamental. If you leave the flower on the plant and allow pollination to occur, a deep orange fruit—the rose hip—will develop. A shrub adorned with rose hips is a sight to behold. Some are tiny and verging on red, others look like mini pumpkins, still others are strangely oblong and squidlike. All contain extremely high levels of vitamins A, C, and E. In fact, rose hips bring shame to citrus fruits, having much more vitamin C gram per gram than oranges. Choosing the right variety is crucial. While all roses should give hips, it's the old style rugosas that have the best flavor. If you have the room, try *Rosa glauca* for an extra ornamental punch. This old rose has blue-tinged foliage and burnished canes; it is exquisite when the elongated orange hips develop in the fall.

How to grow it: Roses don't have to be big pains in the butt—they can be easy. Like most of your other edibles, they want good, rich soil with plenty of amendment, and at least four to five hours of direct sunlight a day. If your roses are spindly, weak, and prone to insect infestation, grow tougher roses, such as floribundas, polyanthas, and rugosas. Smaller roses with fewer petals will integrate better into an edible garden than the prissy hybrid teas or buxom grandifloras—and you won't be as tempted to cut the flowers and sacrifice those wonderful hips. Hardy in zones 4–10.

How to use it: Rose hip tea is the classic preparation: dry the fruit, put it in a tea ball, and steep in hot water. Rose petals are also often used as garnishes and in jellies.

ROSEMARY
Rosmarinus officinalis

Evergreen perennial herb; dark green needlelike leaves with gray reverse tightly packed on woody stems; flower color ranges from light blue to almost purple; shape varies from upright to prostrate to large rambling shrubs; early to mid-summer bloom; size varies.

I can't imagine a garden without rosemary—even a strictly ornamental garden should include it just for appearance alone. (Granted, I live in a climate where rosemary can be used as a hedge material, but it can be appreciated on a smaller scale as well.) All rosemary has semi-woody branches and finely textured deep green leaves. The plants, which almost look like conifers, are easily pruned into shapes—you could have the edible version of small topiary balls in your front yard. The flowers are usually blue, prolific, and drive bees mad. I adore the upright shrubs 'Tuscan Blue' and 'Blue Spires', both of which are bold in flavor but don't have the overt pine-resin overtones common to other cultivars, especially the prostrate ones.

How to grow it: Sun and drainage are the keys to success with rosemary. It doesn't want a rich soil—in fact, the flavor is better if the soil is lean. If you live in an area prone to frost, you can still enjoy rosemary by growing it in a pot. A container will ensure proper drainage (add some gritty sand to your potting mix or use a planting mix for cactus), and you'll be able to bring it inside once the temperatures dip. Potted rosemary looks great whether nestled between plants in a garden or inside near a sunny window during the winter. Its warm fragrance will give you a whiff of summer whenever you walk by. Hardy in zones 7–11.

How to use it: Rosemary and chicken are best friends in the kitchen—they go hand in hand. Use it in breads, when roasting potatoes, or if you are feeling adventurous, in cookies. The fragrance of rosemary is rumored to stimulate the third eye. Try adding some to a warm bath and see if your level of enlightenment rises.

SAGE
Salvia officinalis

....

Perennial herb; gray, green, purple, or variegated leaves; blossoms are purple spikes; small mounding shrublets; summer bloom; 1 1/2 ft. tall × 3 ft. wide.

....

Any edible garden that wants to look good should include this tough herb in its ranks. Regular edible sage, *Salvia officinalis*, is a handsome low mound of gray leaves that also boasts beautiful flowers. You might think you were looking at a variety of ornamental sage if your nose wasn't telling you otherwise—one deep whiff will call up memories of Thanksgiving stuffing and country sausage. Experiment with cultivars that explore the color palette more fully. *S. officinalis* 'Purpurascens' (purple sage) is a very cool collection of purple, gray, and gray-green leaves, and *S. officinalis* 'Icterina' sparkles with green and gold variegation. Speaking of variegation, *S. officinalis* 'Tricolor' does 'Icterina' one better by splashing itself with purple, green, cream, and rose. The granddaddy of sages is *S. officinalis* 'Berggarten', which has big fuzzy gray leaves, a graceful mounding habit, and a full, almost meaty flavor.

How to grow it: Like the other Mediterranean herbs (rosemary, marjoram, oregano, and lavender), sage actually likes lean soil, so don't plant it in amended beds. Tuck sages where you need something tough and they will shine. Give them plenty of sun and not too much water, and they will give you back flavor with a side order of beauty. Perennial in zones 6–10, annual elsewhere.

How to use it: Sage is a fantastic addition to bean soup, stuffing, or bread. You can even fry the leaves and enjoy this herbal chip on its own or as a garnish for pasta or gnocchi.

SHISO
Perilla frutescens

....

Annual herb; green and red leaves; light purple flower spikes; upright, lightly branching habit; early to mid-summer bloom; 18 in. tall × 8 in. wide; 75–85 days to maturity.

....

The fantastic annual herb known as shiso is also referred to as Japanese basil or beefsteak plant—whatever you call it, it is very pretty. I love the purple-leafed variety (*Perilla frutescens* 'Atropurpurea'), but even the green form (*P. frutescens*) really "brings it" in the garden. They both have large leaves with serrated edges that look like they've been cut with pinking shears. Shiso is related to the shade-lover coleus; like coleus, some varieties have leaves splashed with magenta.

How to grow it: Both green and purple shiso grow very easily from seed to about 18 in. tall and about half as wide. Shiso tends to flower quickly where summers are hot, but since all parts of this plant are edible (leaves, blossoms, and stem) you won't lose out.

How to use it: The unique flavor of shiso is a mix of mint and ginger with a basil overtone and a hint of cumin. Shiso is often used in Japanese cooking; the raw leaves are a traditional companion to sushi and sashimi. The leaves also work as a fresh wrap for cooked meats and fish—wrap it around grilled shrimp for a tasty bite.

....

OPPOSITE, TOP LEFT: The first word people associate with roses might not be "edible," but the hips are an incredibly rich source of vitamin C. Photo by Ann Summa

OPPOSITE, TOP RIGHT: A tidy hedge made of procumbent rosemary lines this rock path under a canopy of olive trees. Photo by Ivette Soler

OPPOSITE, BOTTOM LEFT: The pink, purple, and cream colors splashed across the leaves of *Salvia officinalis* 'Tricolor' picks up the vibrant rosy tints of *Echeveria* 'Afterglow'. Photo by Ann Summa

OPPOSITE, BOTTOM RIGHT: Shiso's serrated edges and luminous green color make it attractive enough to use in the garden even if it wasn't edible. Photo by Ann Summa

SORREL
Rumex species

Perennial; green, slender, oval leaves; reddish purple flowers and buds; summer bloom; 16 in. tall and wide.

Many edible gardeners are familiar with green sorrel (*Rumex acetosa*), a staple in European kitchens, and a lovely, tidy, front-of-the-border edible. But when you want real ornamental bang for your buck, reach for the somewhat gruesomely named bloody dock (*R. sanguineus*): the slender, oval, red-veined leaves have a glorious maroon tracery embossed on them. Adding at least one of these to the edible front yard is a must.

How to grow it: Sorrel and bloody dock love moisture; plant in areas where water naturally collects or cluster with other edibles that also enjoy a little extra water. Keeping the bloom spike cut back will help the leaves remain attractive and will also stop it from reseeding excessively (in wet areas of the country its reported to be a bit of a pest). Plant sorrel in the edible garden—rather than at the edge of a pond—and eat this yummy beauty liberally to keep it under control. Hardy in zones 6–10.

How to use it: Add young, colorful leaves of bloody dock to salads for a visual punch and a distinctive lemony, acidic flavor. Sorrel is delicious in soups, as well as in fish and egg dishes. Put finely chopped leaves in salad dressings or mayonnaise for a nice herbal brightness that doesn't overwhelm other flavors.

OPPOSITE, TOP: A highly ornamental version of sorrel, *Rumex sanguineus*, cuddles around the succulent *Aeonium* 'Caitlin'. Photo by Ann Summa

OPPOSITE, BOTTOM: Who can resist a strawberry? Small, juicy globes dangle from a wooden raised bed, begging to be picked and enjoyed. Photo by Ivette Soler

STRAWBERRY
Fragaria species

Perennial; pleated and serrated green foliage; white flowers followed by red berries; mounding habit; late spring to early summer bloom; size varies.

A strawberry patch is pure enchantment. Small mounds of fresh, green, pleated leaves merge together to create a carpet of prettiness, which hides the dangling, ruby-red treasures. A freshly picked strawberry rinsed off by the hose and popped in your mouth while tending to your garden is one of the great pleasures of summer. Plant strawberries in front of the taller denizens of the garden—both edible and ornamental. If allowed to spread, it can create a dense, weed-smothering layer that is as attractive as it is useful.

How to grow it: Once I get strawberries in the ground I let them do their own thing and enjoy wonderful sweet berries, plus a gloriously lush mat of textured leaves. If your strawberry dreams take you down the path of intense cultivation, you can explore techniques to get bigger berries like cutting "daughter plants" away from the "mother." Keep this perennial well fertilized by top dressing with compost during the growing season. If you live in frost zones, mulch well in the winter to prevent root damage. Hardy in zones 4–9.

How to use it: Fresh strawberries are hard to get in the kitchen because they tend to be eaten on the way inside. But if you can do it, your choices are limitless. I would encourage you to serve these little morsels of summer as naked as possible—with a drizzle of balsamic vinegar or maybe some sweetened heavy cream.

SWEET BAY
Laurus nobilis

....

Evergreen, slow-growing tree or shrub; shiny, deep green, elliptic leaves; little yellow flowers; spring bloom; up to 25 ft. tall × 15 ft. wide.

....

Evergreen elements are important to include in an edible front yard garden. A bay tree (or bay hedge) would be a worthwhile investment of time and money—it could be the stable, unchanging backbone to your seasonal edible landscape. Sweet bay is slow growing, but in the right climate it will become a tree over time. Planted side by side, bay plants will form a strong, fragrant, and attractive hedge. Those in cooler zones can still enjoy the dark leaves of this shrubby tree by planting in containers; dot a few around the garden and bring them in when it gets wintry cold. Select attractive containers to add a decorative dimension to your front yard.

How to grow it: Fertile, well-drained soil is the name of the game for this easy-to-grow shrubby tree. Be sure to get your bay from a reputable source—other plants that are less useful in the kitchen easily masquerade as *Laurus nobilis*. Patience is definitely a virtue when you are growing bay: it will grow slowly but surely. Hardy to zone 8.

How to use it: Bay leaves are fragrant when bruised, and add a distinct flavor to Mediterranean cooking. One bay leaf is all you need for soups, stews, or braises. Just clip a leaf off as you need it. You can also strew dried leaves around your pantry to ward off moths and other insects.

THYME
Thymus species

....

Perennial herb; gray-green, green, or white and yellow variegated foliage; pink or white flowers; habit varies from flat groundcover to mounding; summer bloom; 1–12 in. tall.

....

Imagine several different varieties of thyme planted together in a colorful herbal carpet—what could be a more beautiful way to finish the garden than with this hard-working herb that appears so delicate? I swoon over lime thyme (*Thymus ×citriodorus* 'Lime') which has the brightest light green color; woolly thyme (*T. pseudolanuginosus*), a soft gray, creeping groundcover that is almost completely flat with a furry texture; and 'Golden Lemon' thyme (*Thymus ×citriodorus* 'Golden Lemon'), a beautiful plant whose small leaves are midgreen ringed with bright gold. It is hard to go wrong with this exquisite herb. You'll soon find the thyme you love the most. Or you may decide that you just can't decide and the central theme in your front yard could be a vibrant, jazzy thyme collection.

How to grow it: Keep thyme happy with lots of sun and lean soil (rich soil and shade weaken the color and flavor of this tough-as-nails plant). Cut and use often or it will become tough and woody. Hardy in zones 4–9.

How to use it: A celebrity chef I admire starts every savory dish with a sprig of thyme in the bottom of the pan. It's a good idea—thyme needs long cooking to mellow out its assertive flavor. It adds distinctiveness to meat dishes, whether chicken, beef, or pork. Try different thyme varieties with different dishes and find the best combination.

....

OPPOSITE: Thyme is an important part of the ornamental edible palette. There are dozens of varieties in different colors and forms that help to knit together the front of your planting beds, providing the all-important groundcover layer. Photo by Ann Summa

dreams vs. reality:
edibles to think twice about planting in front

The front yard edible garden should be a place that gives us food without extraordinary effort, and choosing unfussy, enthusiastic plants is a big part of making that happen. We who love growing food think *all* plants that feed us are beautiful, but the reality is that some need a careful vetting before being included in your front yard. Remember rule number one—the entire plant must look great for the entire season. With that in mind, here are a few plants to consider placing elsewhere if at all possible.

Carrots. I adore carrots but they give little, ornamentally speaking, to the front yard edible garden besides their green and ferny tops. Maximize the space carrots would occupy by planting lettuce, beets, or chard, all of which deliver knockout visual and culinary punches.

Cauliflower. Cauliflower is simply too picky: it needs a long, cool growing season (no frost, no heat), and to achieve the desired tight, snowball head it must be blanched (which means tying the outer leaves over the forming head and leaving it that way through the growing season). In addition, you will have to battle the pests that attack all brassicas.

Cucurbits: cucumbers, gourds, melons, squash, and watermelons. Consider planting all members of the cucurbit clan in your backyard or another less-visible space—it is hard to keep these plants looking good. (It is also really hard to make a pumpkin patch look well designed.) Even the best varieties are susceptible to powdery mildew: the coarse leaves look fantastic at first but will inevitably become yellow and mildewed. If you do plant cucurbits, cut the affected leaves the minute you see a hint of mildew, and make certain that the air circulation is free flowing.

Tomatoes. Yes, the mighty tomato may not be the best edible to plant in the front yard. The wonderful heirlooms that have such magnificent taste and lovely fruits also tend to be big, rangy plants that can easily go all over the place. Even with tomato cages, spirals, and other supports, tomatoes can look ungainly. Being such heavy feeders, their leaves can begin to wear out during the peak of the season, and crunchy, yellow foliage is to be avoided in the front yard. However, I do think small or cherry tomatoes ('Sungold' and 'Green Zebra' in particular) can be charming when they cascade over a bed or peak in between other plants. So use discretion and make your choices wisely if you desire tomatoes out front.

In the event that you decide your front yard is the only place for your "forbidden foods," pay special attention to your hardscape. Cucumbers, squash and zucchini can look perfectly lush in a well-designed raised bed (with good air circulation) and tomatoes can be reined in by handsome cages and selective pruning. If you can, place them in areas that aren't easily visible so your front yard edible garden will appear neat and fresh.

OPPOSITE: Tomatoes can easily grow large and rangy. Giving extra thought to their support will help them look attractive in your front yard. Photo by Ann Summa

three

EXPANDING OUR EDIBLE PALETTE
the helpers

When designing the front yard, it's crucial to create an ornamental backbone onto which you can drape your edible dreams. **Most of the plants that give us food are annuals, and the shrubs and trees that give us berries and fruit are rarely evergreen. If the front yard garden, a space in public view, is exclusively edible, the landscape might look fallow for up to half of the year. By expanding the traditional edible palette to include ornamental plants we can add strength, structure, and year-round interest to our gardens. There is no reason for horticultural segregation: the eclectic mixing of edibles and ornamentals makes for tougher, healthier gardens.**

The plants listed in this chapter do not encompass, by any stretch of the imagination, the only non-edibles to integrate into your front yard food landscape. When choosing these ornamental helpers, I focused on beautiful plants that are not purely decorative—many have a historical use in productive gardens. Some plants are traditional medicinals or used for brewing teas; some are useful for attracting pollinators and other beneficial insects; others have been used in the past to make fiber or crafts. Even if you won't be making sisal or nectar from agaves, gin from junipers, or flax from phormiums, these plants will expand your palette of choices, give you more to play with, and add another layer of interest to your garden.

AGAVE
Agave species

Perennial; green, gray, blue, or variegated color; succulent rosettes with stiff, spearlike leaves; size varies.

It is thrilling that these incredible plants have become popular in landscape design circles. Most people don't have enough room for giant agaves, but many medium to small agaves are a desirable size for the front yard edible garden. *Agave americana* 'Mediopicta Alba' grows to 3 ft. tall and has spiny gray leaves accentuated with a central white stripe—it's a little clownish but in the best possible way. 'Blue Glow' agave boasts a perfect 16 in. × 16 in. arrangement of steel blue leaves with magenta edges that catch the afternoon sun. If you want to go big and bold, look no further than *A. weberi*, which is 5 ft. × 4 ft. and quite sturdy, but still presents itself like a prima ballerina. There is a color and arrangement of leaf to entice any gardener to plant one, or even ten, in their front yard. Don't be scared off by their sharp spikes, they may be a little prickly, but agaves are pussycats. Once you experience the sculptural drama they bring to your garden, you'll be a devotee.

How to grow it: Sun is essential. In the hottest zones, tender agaves like *Agave attenuata* (foxtail agave) or *A. vilmoriniana* (octopus agave) will happily live in dappled shade, but most agaves need bright sun to prosper. It isn't only hot zone gardeners that can enjoy the glories of agaves—some hardy agaves can tolerate freezing temperatures (with a little TLC, of course). If you live in a cold climate, plant agaves in a bright location where they can bask in reflected light. They need sharp drainage and careful watering: too much will rot them (especially in cooler climates), too little will stress them. If you find the place that is just right, you can find success. Hardy in zones 9–11, hardy blue agaves zones 5–10.

How to use it: The traditional uses for agaves are numerous. Their fibers were harvested to make sisal for rope, the underground bulb is used to make mescal and tequila, and recently the nectar of the agave plant has been heralded as a low-glycemic sweetener.

PREVIOUS PAGE: Cool, silver *Artemisia* 'Powis Castle' is softly caressed by a gray artichoke leaf. This duo shyly peeks though a haze of parsley flowers. Photo by Ann Summa

OPPOSITE: Using a variety of ornamental helpers, like agaves and euphorbias, gives your garden strength and eclecticism. Photo by Ann Summa

ALOE
Aloe vera

Perennial; light green leaves; yellow flowers; rosette, clump-forming succulent; spring to early summer bloom; 20 in. tall and wide.

Many people have a pot of *Aloe vera* growing near the kitchen for burns and scrapes; take it out front and see what great contrasts of form and texture occur when mixed with the soft shapes of edibles in the garden. It has a similar sculptural profile as agave, but has yearly blooms as a bonus. If you live in a frost-free zone and want to delve into the world of aloes, dive in. There are groundcover aloes, tree aloes, and an aloe for any garden situation in between.

How to grow it: These succulents are tender and can't handle frost. In cold zones, plant aloe in a pot that you can move indoors. When planting aloe in the ground, amend the soil with chipped granite or coarse sand. This improves drainage and ensures that it will bloom. Poor drainage is death to aloes; the leaves are already more than 90 percent water and they can't handle moisture standing around their roots. Hardy in zones 9–11.

How to use it: Aloe vera is a well-known healing salve for wounds, burns, and skin irritations. Its thick, gooey innards are also very moisturizing and can be slathered on your face while relaxing in a warm bath—a beauty treatment straight from your front yard.

ANGELICA
Angelica species

Biennial; green or purple foliage; large, green or purple flowers; summer through fall bloom; 5–6 ft. tall × 3 ft. wide.

Angelica, the "angel of herbs," is said to have magical, healing properties. While that may or may not be true, the fact that it is a stunning plant is undeniable. Angelica is lush, dramatic, and even a little beguiling. The pure green *Angelica archangelica*, and the brooding, purple-tinged, witchy *A. gigas*, will both stop traffic outside your front door with their dramatic flowers that bloom in large, domed umbels.

How to grow it: The angelica twins love moderate temperatures and fertile, moist soil. Plant it in areas of your front yard where water naturally collects and you won't need to provide supplemental water. If you can, plant angelica from seed in the fall—it will leaf out in the spring and you may get blooms that summer. Hardy in zones 4–9.

How to use it: Angelica is edible, but is such a glorious plant that most are loath to harvest it. The stems and leaves have an herbal, celery-like flavor, and the root is used to flavor liquors.

ARTEMISIA OR WORMWOOD
Artemisia species

Perennial; gray-green or silver foliage on woody plants; small, yellow flowers in some varieties; rangy, mounding sub-shrubs; size varies.

Artemisia absinthium is the specific species used to make the hallucinogenic liqueur but the entire genus of plants is visually intoxicating. *Artemisia* 'Powis Castle' is a vision of pure silver, with delicately filigreed leaves that act as a perfect foil for all of the green in an edible garden. These plants also lend textural interest to the landscape: the leaves of all varieties have some degree of serration, from slightly pinked edges to leaves that almost look like they've been laser cut.

How to grow it: The only hard part is keeping artemisia from looking leggy and rangy. A strong hand with the pruners is needed to pinch it back and keep it full. Good drainage and bright sun are essential. Hardy in zones 3–9.

How to use it: If you are feeling adventurous, try your hand at making absinthe. Or, if you'd rather avoid the moonshine game, you can easily make an insect repellent spray. Heat about 4 ounces of crushed artemisia leaves and a quart of water in an old saucepan (one not used for cooking food). Slowly bring the leaves and water to a rolling boil, then remove from heat and let cool overnight. Strain the leaves out and then use a funnel to decant into a spray bottle. Add 5 drops of liquid castile soap to the bottle and shake well. Spray this concoction on the undersides of tender leaves where the caterpillars of the white cabbage moth like to lurk and chew.

BOX
Buxus species

Evergreen shrub; small green leaves; yellow flowers; early spring bloom; size varies.

Yes, in many ways box, or boxwood, is what I've been railing against—it is *the* foundation plant. Box is almost as ubiquitously planted as sod, plopped in front of a house without a second thought. But this traditional hedging material for parterres and potagers is no old fashioned has-been. Few things are as charming and tidy as a vegetable bed enclosed by a box hedge.

How to grow it: Box grows well in cool, moist conditions, but it demands good drainage to flourish. Plant it a little high so that the crown doesn't sink below the soil level as it settles. Since this shrub relies on the beauty of its tiny green leaves, you can feel confident giving it a little extra nitrogen (maybe top dress with well-rotted manure) to prevent it from looking faded in the sun. Hardy in zones 5–8.

How to use it: While box has long been used as a medicinal herb to stimulate and detoxify, it is best not to make tea or tonic out of it as it can interact with other drugs and have adverse effects. Enjoy the tidy, formal look that box gives to your edible garden.

CATMINT
Nepeta faassenii

Perennial; small gray-green leaves; white to pale blue flowers; spreading sub shrubby habit; summer to fall bloom; 3 ft. tall and wide.

You don't have to be a feline to enjoy this member of the mint family. Grow this sprawling plant as an easy, drought-tolerant groundcover—it does a great job of connecting taller plants with the smaller, front-of-the-border choices. A word of warning: you might not want this plant if you have a large feral cat population. (Though, on the other hand, cats hanging around your garden keep other varmints in check.)

How to grow it: Unfussy catmint is almost too easy to grow. Plant it in a location that you didn't get around to amending and it will thank you by growing rapidly and blooming profusely. Hardy in zones 3–9.

How to use it: The volatile oils that give cats that euphoric, half-crazed reaction have an effect on us, too. For humans, catmint is a mild soporific—a sleep aid and nerve tonic— when ingested as a tea.

CLEVELAND SAGE
Salvia clevelandii

Tender perennial herb; greenish gray leaves; brittle stems; blue flowers arranged in whorls up the bloomstalk; summer to fall bloom; 3 ft. tall and wide.

This spectacular variety of sage demands special attention. It is a pure pleasure to observe in the garden: as it grows, the mounding habit morphs naturally into an even, rounded shape. Some Cleveland sages can be a little large for the average front yard, but compact 'Winifred Gilman' is easily incorporated into a smaller garden. This handsome plant has small, greenish-gray leaves on dark stems, whorls of blue flowers stacked one on top of the other, and the freshest scent of any salvia. Its clean, herbal, piney fragrance practically lowers the temperature with its cooling freshness. Plant it next to your mailbox or front door (or anywhere that you'll brush by it daily) and you'll be instantly invigorated with its bright perfume.

How to grow it: All sages need sharp drainage and lean soil (fertile soil will cause floppy, overly lush growth that will make the top of the plant heavy and can cause the brittle stems to break in the center). To keep plants fresh and tight, cut back *Salvia clevelandii* by 1/3 after blooming. While pruning can be a chore, the incomparable scent makes cutting this salvia almost a treat. Hardy in zones 8–10.

How to use it: Cleveland sage is a powerful attractor of bees and hummingbirds; plant it in your edible garden and entice pollinators to linger. That lively, clean fragrance just begs to be used in the bath, in sachets, and even as incense.

DAYLILY
Hemerocallis species

Perennial; green, grassy foliage with stiff, green scapes; lily-like flowers in a vast range of colors; clump-forming habit; late spring bloom; size varies.

While bloom alone is never enough reason to include a plant in a garden, the flowers of daylilies make a powerful argument to do just that. The range of flower color gives you an almost endless palette: you can choose from the pimento zip of bright red daylilies, the soft watercolor wash of pinks, or the bass note of maroon—and that just scratches the surface. Thankfully, we don't have to worry about the rest of the plant not adding to our design. The grassy leaves are just as valuable for their textural contrast against the similar foliage of many edible plants. The arching sword-shaped leaves of daylilies grow in large clumps, like an ornamental grass, and can be used as a repetitive motif to draw the eye through the garden.

How to grow it: Plant in compost-amended soil in a sunny spot, and you will get fountains of grassy leaves as well as spectacular flowers. While daylilies can deal with short periods of drought, regular water ensures better blooms. Cut off any yellowing foliage right away to keep these plants looking their best. I enjoy the ritual of going through the garden right before sunset and breaking off the spent flowers, which I add to my compost. This allows for the next day's flowers to show themselves off without a wilted friend behind them tarnishing their shine. Hardy in zones 3–10.

How to use it: Daylily rhizomes have been used for centuries in China as a mild diuretic. The flowers are also edible; try them dipped in batter and fried. Of course, eating them requires sacrificing the exquisite blooms, but maybe you can dedicate one day of blossoms for a special dinner.

ELDERBERRY
Sambucus species

Shrub or small tree; leaves green, chartreuse, or purple, deeply cut and filigreed; flowers are lacy white umbels; upright, open, shrubby habit; early summer bloom; size varies.

Elderberry is one of the most elegant shrubs around. One of my top picks, *Sambucus racemosa* 'Sutherland Gold', boasts deeply cut golden leaves that contrast beautifully with the green foliage of most edibles. Those attracted to the dark side will be drawn to *Sambucus nigra* 'Black Lace' and its sooty, filigreed leaves. These majestic specimen plants can create wonderful spotlight moments in your front yard.

How to grow it: Elderberry loves water so it would be a serious challenge to grow it in drier areas of the country. While it will tolerate some shade, it needs sun to develop good leaf color. This rangy shrub should be cut back hard once a year to give it a fuller profile. Hardy in zones 4–8.

How to use it: This plant has magical associations: ingesting elderberries supposedly brings on the power to see the future. If that's true then we must have many clairvoyant birds flitting about because our feathered friends love the small black berries. If you can grab them before the birds, try your hand at elderberry jam or even elderberry wine.

EUPHORBIA OR SPURGE
Euphorbia species

Perennial; green, gray, or purple foliage; chartreuse, gold, purple, or red flowers (really bracts); mainly early spring bloom; size varies.

Euphorbias are valuable supporting players in the cast of characters that inhabit the front yard edible garden. The foliage makes a powerful statement with its linear leaves climbing up straight, unbranching stems, but the blooms are the real scene stealers. *Euphorbia wulfenii*, whose domes of chartreuse coin-like flowers are thrillingly martian, never fails to elicit comments from passersby. Some varieties of euphorbia are variegated, some have rich purple leaves, and others boast steely blue foliage. The forms of this plant run the gamut from tidy little mounds to large shrubs.

How to grow it: This is another easy helper that gives and gives, and all it needs from you is a home. Plant in sun or shade, and even dry shade—which is famously hard to deal with in a garden—and euphorbias will take it all in stride. While these plants will withstand drought and thrive in a dry garden, they look much better when irrigated. Hardy in zones 7–10.

How to use it: Important: euphorbia is not edible. The "poisonous" milky sap is an irritant similar to latex (those who have latex allergies will likely be sensitive to euphorbias). The sap can cause a rash to develop and can be painful if it gets into your eyes. Euphorbia is included in the helper palette because it is exactly that—a helper—not only ornamentally but also as a companion for warding off gophers. Until you've experienced a gopher problem you have no idea the amount of damage these tunneling creatures can inflict. A plant whose roots discourage them is one I definitely want in my front yard edible garden.

FOXTAIL FERN
Asparagus densiflorus 'Meyersii'

Perennial; bright green twisting fronds covered with needle-like ferny foliage; tiny white flowers; red berries; mid- to late summer bloom, usually inconspicuous; 2 ft. tall × 3 ft. wide.

Due to the revived appreciation of unusual plants that evoke a Dr. Seuss vibe, the almost out-of-fashion foxtail fern is staging a comeback. Whimsical, twisting and turning, cylindrical "arms" reach out and try to touch the nearby plants. These octopus-like fronds are densely clothed with tiny leaves, giving the plant a fluffy, soft appearance and making foxtail fern an excellent textural companion to many front yard edibles. Its bright green, odd form encourages you to cut loose and play with the possibilities of plant combining.

How to grow it: This isn't really and truly a fern. Like agave it's a member of the lily family, and is similarly quite tough and drought tolerant. That crisp green color needs very little water to maintain, but regular garden water will create a luxurious mound of green, fluffy foxtails. Flexibility is its middle name—sun or shade, rain or drought, poor soil or amended—this funny plant will win you over with reliability. Hardy in zones 9 and higher, zone 8 with protection.

How to use it: Take advantage of the open structure and interesting texture of foxtail fern by planting it with edibles that have lax habits—it could be a natural support for snap peas, for instance. Its fountain shape also leaves room at the base to accommodate smaller edibles like lettuces or sages.

GERANIUM (SCENTED)
Pelargonium species

....

Perennial often grown as an annual; green to gray-green leaves; white or pink flowers; shape varies from small mounds to sprawling groundcovers to rangy upright pseudo-shrubs; summer bloom; size varies.

....

These wonderfully fragrant and superbly tactile cottage garden standbys (and plant collector's dream) fit in well within a front yard edible garden. *Pelargonium tomentosum* (peppermint-scented geranium) has soft, fuzzy leaves that just beg to be touched. Choose from a big range of plant types: some grow naturally into small puffs, others are rangy and spread into ground-covering masses, and yet others are stiffly upright. Leaves range from tiny and scalloped (*P.* 'Nutmeg') to the large oak-leaf *P.* 'Chocolate Mint' (which also has a big maroon splotch in the center) to the intensely dissected *P. graveolens*. This wonderful world of leafy beauties provides plenty of options for our edible gardens.

How to grow it: If you live in a cooler climate, take cuttings of your plants at the end of the growing season, propagate them (easily done in a glass of water), then pot them up and keep them on a sunny windowsill until the warmth of summer beckons you outside again. Perennial in zones 10–11, annual in zones 4–9.

How to use it: The volatile oils that give pelargoniums their scent makes them great flavoring agents in vinegars, teas, and other drinks (try the rose-scented kind for an amazing rose-y lemonade). The leaves can also be used in jellies or scented sugars, or candied for sweet garnishes. When I buy a new novel, I often repurpose a leaf of my 'Chocolate Mint' as a fragrant bookmark.

HOPS
Humulus lupulus

....

Perennial; green pleated foliage; papery, bract-encrusted flowers; late spring bloom.

....

Even though you may not harvest your hops to make beer, grow this vine for the ornamental power it wields. *Humulus lupulus* 'Aurea' is a sight to behold. Golden pleated leaves seem to glow with their own light. And then there are the green flowers—hanging papery lanterns of chartreuse bracts that flutter in the wind. Be still my beating heart.

How to grow it: This is a fabulous vine but beware, it can take over the world. Give hops fertile soil (it is all leaf and papery bracts so it can handle extra nitrogen). The trick to controlling this easy grower is being unafraid to cut it. Thinning the vine will also ward off mildew by improving the air circulation. Hardy in zones 3–8.

How to use it: Make beer! Or, if you'd rather not explore the murky depths of home brewing, try adding some hops flowers to your tea and take advantage of the softly sedative properties. The tea will probably taste better with some honey or sugar since the flowers can be a bit bitter.

....

OPPOSITE, TOP LEFT: *Asparagus densiflorus* 'Meyersii' is an oldie but goodie. Its fluffy fronds twist and turn, weaving in and out of neighboring plants, making friends with whatever it sits near. Photo by Ivette Soler

OPPOSITE, TOP RIGHT: Hops have interesting, papery flowers, and grow well in shady situations. These ones are bound for beer brewing. Photo by Ann Summa. Garden of Eric Knutzen and Kelly Coyne

OPPOSITE, BOTTOM: Well-chosen and appropriately sized junipers make excellent helpers for edible plantings. Photo by Ivette Soler

JUNIPER
Juniperus species

....

Evergreen conifer; green, blue-green, or yellow foliage; size varies from groundcover to tree but all have tiny, needle-like leaves.

....

Some will balk when they see the ubiquitous, lowly juniper included in this list. It's understandable—junipers are often planted as a thoughtless mass and then left to get huge, woody, ratty, and full of spider webs. However, junipers are ubiquitous for good reason. These workhorses thrive in a wide variety of climates, and, when properly planted and maintained, they look great. Junipers help to create textural shifts, can be used in multiples to create rhythm, and are unassuming supporting players, happily giving the spotlight to others. Don't overlook this plant just because it is common—let it work for you.

How to grow it: Even though junipers are famously unfussy, you will have better luck if you give them a home in amended garden soil. Many plant guides will tell you that junipers require full sun, but they are actually good choices for dappled shade, especially in hotter parts of the country. Pay close attention to the mature size of the variety you choose—their misuse is often due to being shoved into too small spaces and then cut to fit. Junipers do not take well to shearing; the natural shape is ruined, and they are slow to grow back from old wood. Choose the right variety and you will be happy with this attractive structural shrub. Hardy in zones 4–9.

How to use it: Juniper is a flavoring component in gin, and the astringent berries are used to spice meats. The berries are also an effective diuretic, and may help ease the pain of gout.

....

OPPOSITE: The candelabra effect of a flowering mullein is enhanced by the early morning light. Photo by Ann Summa

LAVENDER
Lavandula species

....

Perennial herb; green to gray foliage; flowers in wands from pink to blue to purple; late spring through fall bloom; size varies.

....

Lavender is a top notch ornamental companion for the edible landscape. The right lavender in the right zone can make a wonderful, fragrant hedge, and the silvery leaves of many varieties present an opportunity to create important color contrasts. *Lavandula ×intermedia* 'Grosso' and *L. ×intermedia* 'Provence', both grown commercially by the perfume industry for oil and flowers, are exquisite. These plants are big and bold and need to be kept in line, like ambitious chorus girls. You may prefer the smaller, tidier look of the English lavenders such as *L. angustifolia* 'Hidcote' and *L. angustifolia* 'Munstead'. With so many species and varieties to explore, there is truly a lavender for every garden.

How to grow it: Drainage, drainage, and more drainage. Lavender doesn't need to be kept completely dry but it does need its soil to wick the water away from its roots. Plant lavender in lean, sharp soil so it grows tight rather than excessively lush and floppy. This may mean siting your lavender in the unamended or lightly amended parts of your front yard. Keep your pruners handy if you live in a climate with a long, warm growing season—these exuberant Mediterranean plants might try to muscle in on their neighbors. Depending on the species, hardy in zones 5–10.

How to use it: Lavender is a medicinal herb and is used in cooking more now than ever before. Don't be afraid of lavender in your savory food. It's a staple in the Herbes de Provence spice blend, used as a rub on meats and in sauces. Lavender in sweet preparations, like cookies and sherbet, is more palatable for most. Growing your own lavender gives you an endless supply for potpourri, tub tea, and closet sachets.

MARIGOLDS
Tagetes species

Perennial; olive green foliage with simple, orange-gold flowers; late summer to late fall bloom; 3–4 ft. tall × 2–5 ft. wide.

Perennial marigolds are quite different from the big-headed annual flowers. They grow larger and wilder, and tiny, golden, daisy-shaped flowers adorn the fragrant shrubs. The smaller species, *Tagetes lucida* (Spanish tarragon) is used in cooking, while rambling *T. lemmonii* (copper canyon daisy), is known for its pungent, minty scent. Some people love the smell, some people hate it. I guess it's the same way with bugs since this shrubby herbaceous perennial can both attract and repel insects—bees love the flowers, and the nasties stay away from it and whatever you have planted nearby.

How to grow it: Grow this easy-care plant in average garden soil with regular water. It withstands drought, and bounces back from freezes. *Tagetes lemmonii* can become gargantuan without regular pruning. Just make sure not to prune it too far into fall, or you will delay the glorious winter bloom. Hardy in zones 8–11.

How to use it: Spanish tarragon is an excellent substitute for French tarragon; it has a less peppery, more licorice-like flavor and is delicious in teas and herbal spice blends. Strew the leaves of *Tagetes lemmonii* in cupboards to repel insects.

MULLEIN
Verbascum species

Biennial; green or gray leaves form a dense rosette in the first season and a bloomspike in the next season; flowers often yellow; summer bloom; 70 in. tall × 23 in. wide.

It is high time these old-fashioned cottage beauties made their way back into our beds. Mullein is an interesting biennial: the first year it sports a cabbage-like arrangement of big, felty leaves, and the second year it springs up into a candelabra of majestic proportions. Try *Verbascum bombyciferum* for the extra ornamental appeal of white fuzzy buds that burst open into yellow flowers.

How to grow it: Mullein tolerates most soils, from clay to sandy. It is easily grown from seed, so easy, in fact, that after the first bloom you will be finding its first year rosettes all around your front yard. Hardy in zones 5–9.

How to use it: The flowers and stamens of mullein are traditionally used in teas for coughs and sore throats. It is also said to be relaxing and helpful in soothing jangled nerves.

MYRTLE
Myrtus communis 'Compacta'

Evergreen shrub; small green leaves; white flowers; small, slow-growing, compact habit; mid-summer bloom; 2–3 ft. tall and wide.

Myrtle shrubs often substitute for boxwood in warmer climates. The overall look is formal—small, closely packed, pointy leaves and fragrant white flowers that bristle with stamens—even when allowed to grow in its natural form. It takes very well to shearing and is a wonderful choice for small hedges and parterres. Plant myrtle in your front yard as a barrier between your edible garden and the sidewalk. Just the small visual cue of a hedge may be enough to keep sticky fingers away from your food.

How to grow it: Myrtle likes sun and regular (but not too much) water. Once established, it practically takes care of itself, just top dress with compost once a year to give it a boost, and lightly shear it after bloom. Hardy in zones 8–10.

How to use it: This shrub has a rich herbal lore, said to endow the person that plants it with good luck and long hair. Myrtle, sacred to the goddess Venus, is traditionally used in bridal bouquets.

OPPOSITE, TOP: The flowers of *Nicotiana alata* 'Lime Green' are delightful. The leaves and roots are also reputed to repel insects. Photo by Ivette Soler

OPPOSITE, BOTTOM: The matte black leaves of the ornamental sweet potato vine (*Ipomoea batatas* 'Ace of Spades') weave and frolic with pequin peppers that are turning black: a colorful visual dialog between neighbors. Photo by Ann Summa

NICOTIANA OR FLOWERING TOBACCO
Nicotiana species

Annuals or perennials grown as annuals; green or gray-ish foliage; red, pink, white, or green flowers; late spring to summer bloom; size varies.

Flowering tobacco earns its place in the edible front yard with its big, rough leaves and nodding flowers that last and last. *Nicotiana alata* 'Lime Green' and *N. langsdorfii* are favorites because of their chic green blossoms, and the long, elegant flowers of *N. sylvestris* 'Only the Lonely' turn the entire plant into a languid sylph. The flowers add a whimsical gracefulness to every planting, and are especially welcome around edibles because they are said to repel voracious insects.

How to grow it: There is nothing to growing this plant—either scatter the seeds or buy small starts from your local nursery. It grows in any soil, and does well in sunny or dappled conditions. Hardy in zones 5–11.

How to use it: Don't smoke it—plant nicotiana in your front yard to help in the war against garden pests, and to enjoy the unusual, attractive flowers.

ORNAMENTAL SWEET POTATO
Ipomoea batatas

Perennial; long, trailing foliage, sometimes heart-shaped or deeply lobed; color ranges from chartreuse to black to copper-blushed, or variegated white, pink, and green; 16 in. tall and spreading.

Ornamental sweet potato vines are foliage plants of the highest order: some have deeply lobed leaves as black as coal, others display bright chartreuse foliage that seems to glow with inner light—and that is just the beginning. New leaf colors and shapes are springing up all the time, each of which is a wonderful addition to the edible front yard. If you have raised beds, take advantage of how this plant drapes languidly over the sides, or let it ramble among other plants. The tuber that this vine grows from is technically edible, but it is large and bitter rather than delicious. Let this sweet potato be a helper—it wants to be beautiful for you.

How to grow it: Ipomoea batatas is a slow starter; it needs summer heat to start putting on a show. But once that show starts: watch out. This vine will grow and grow, and even moderate garden water will cause a lush explosion of gorgeous foliage. Sometimes there can be too much of a good thing—keep your ornamental sweet potato vine in check by selective pruning so it doesn't smother other edibles. If this vine isn't reliably perennial in your zone, take stem cuttings at the end of the growing season and propagate them indoors for the next year. Hardy in zones 8–11.

How to use it: It is a spiller, it is a filler, and it is a thriller—there is nothing ornamental sweet potato vines can't do in the garden. Creating exciting color combinations is easy when you have this plant in your back pocket.

PHORMIUM OR NEW ZEALAND FLAX
Phormium species

Perennial; green, red, or variegated foliage; sword-shaped leaves in upright, arching, or semi-arching clusters; summer bloom, when applicable; size varies.

When garden designers prattle on and on about structural, architectural plants, phormiums are probably front and center in their mind's eye. Sword-shaped leaves, painted in a glorious rainbow of colors, reach for the sky. All varieties can create rhythm and definition in a landscape: large varieties are like watchful sentinels, medium-sized ones are perfect for middle-of-the-border focal points, and smaller ones are fantastic when scattered or ribboned through the garden. If phormiums are out of your zonal reach, grow them in containers—two flanking the entrance to your house would be perfect guardsmen.

How to grow it: Phormiums will flourish once established but sometimes getting them there can be a little rough. Perfect drainage is crucial to their success. Plant them a little higher than the soil line so they won't end up below ground once they settle. To prevent phormiums from falling prey to crown rot, keep the crowns dry and free of soil and debris. Hardy in zones 8–11.

How to use it: Phormiums were used as a source of fiber by the Maori in New Zealand, but don't destroy those amazing leaves—let them do their work in the garden.

PINEAPPLE GUAVA
Feijoa selloana

Evergreen shrub or small tree; gray leaves; shell-pink flowers that are darker on the inside with large stamens; summer bloom; 10–15 ft. tall and wide.

This is a large shrub or small tree with spoon-shaped gray leaves that have a white flocking beneath. The flowers and fruit are edible, but they are tender for most parts of the country. If you can grow them, you'll have an evergreen tree that gives you great color all year and unusual blossoms that look like tiny pink passionflowers.

How to grow it: Give pineapple guava well-composted soil and regular, even water, and you will be pleasantly surprised by this trouble-free fruit tree. It can withstand short periods of drought but fruiting will suffer if deprived of water for too long. Hardy in zones 8–11.

How to use it: Jams and jellies made from guava are scrumptious.

PINEAPPLE SAGE
Salvia elegans

Perennial; light green leaves and scarlet flowers; sprawling habit; late summer to fall bloom; 4 ft. tall × 3 ft. wide.

Pineapple sage is a big girl but that doesn't mean we don't want to play with her—just keep the pruners handy. This is an excellent go-to plant when you want something that will get big fast, perhaps if you are waiting for a fruit tree to grow in and you need to anchor the space. The light green leaves are edible and have a subtle hint of pineapple. The shockingly red flowers are such an eye-singeing color this plant just can't be ignored.

How to grow it: This subtropical salvia appreciates fertile soil, a good amount of water, and dappled light conditions. This is a fast grower: giving it a cutback in early July will keep it from becoming floppy. If pineapple sage is too tender for your zone, you can grow it as an annual. While it may not reach its full stature, it will easily become a big plant in one season. Cut it back to above the crown, dig it up, pot it, and take it inside at the end of the season. Put it in a cool, bright place, keep it moist, and it will be ready to pop back into your garden for the next growing season. Hardy in zones 8–11.

How to use it: Take advantage of the yummy, sweetly complex leaves by adding them to tea (hot or iced). Or go crazy and muddle the leaves for a pineapple sage mojito. The flowers are a colorful addition to any fruit salad.

ST. JOHN'S WORT
Hypericum androsaemum

Herbaceous perennial; deep green leaves; bright yellow flowers; berries in a range of colors; shrubby habit; mid-spring to early summer bloom, berries in fall; 3 ft. tall × 2 ft. wide.

This flowering shrub's pleasing shape, cheerful yellow flowers, and vigorous history as an herbal remedy land it effortlessly on the helper palette. But St. John's wort has something extra—after flowering, the most vivid, exquisite berries appear (in a range of warm colors hugged by maroon-tinged bracts). The *Hypericum* 'Mystical' series is made up of plants that offer orange, red, pink, and even black berries. The tiny fruits have elevated this plant to one of the darlings of the floral trade.

How to grow it: St. John's wort grows well in average, evenly moist soil. It tolerates shade but the best flowers are produced when planted in a sunny location. This shrub flowers on new growth, so it is important to prune it in early spring so you don't sacrifice potential flowers and berries. Hardy in zones 4–9.

How to use it: Harvest the flowers and tender leaves to make a soothing herbal tea. The taste is bitter so mix it with mint and honey for a more palatable drink. Cut a few berry branches and bring them inside to make a lovely and long-lasting floral arrangement.

SUNFLOWERS
Helianthus annuus

Annual; flower colors range from traditional yellow to blazing red; habit and size varies from dwarf to mammoth, single-stemmed to branching; mid- to late summer bloom; 60–90 days to maturity.

Sunflowers are the epitome of the summer garden flower. Large and cheerful, they seem to capture the sunlight and give it right back in a condensed version that doesn't burn our retinas. Sunflowers are also powerful helpers in the edible garden—they magnetically attract bees, the sturdy stems are perfect supports for vining crops, and the seeds are wonderful food for wildlife. Sunflowers are especially worthwhile if you have little gardeners in the family—kids will cultivate a sense of pride and accomplishment by taking care of these undemanding flowers.

How to grow it: I challenge you to find a plant easier to grow from seed than sunflowers. Find a location in full sun, push a seed into soil, sprinkle it with water, and let nature do the hard work. Soon you'll have sprouts, and within a couple of weeks the teenaged plants will grow tall and lanky, reaching for the sky. Sunflowers flourish in average garden soil, though larger varieties do appreciate the added nutrients of compost. Annual in all zones.

How to use it: Tall sunflowers are my personal preference; I think smaller varieties are a wasted opportunity for vertical interest in the edible front yard. Let them support your pole beans, and don't forget that the flowers come in a range of colors—a swath of tall burgundy sunflowers will make a powerful statement in the midsummer garden.

SWEET WOODRUFF
Gallium odoratum

Perennial; small, green, palmlike leaves; dainty white flowers; spreading groundcover; spring bloom; 6–12 in. tall.

Sweet woodruff is a popular groundcover for the shadier areas of the garden, and can be well utilized to carpet spots in which most edibles won't grow well. Some might consider sweet woodruff a bit too aggressive, but since it grows in places where other plants have trouble I wouldn't dismiss it out of hand. For such a tough plant, its appearance is quite dainty—the small leaves, unique for a groundcover, look like tiny palm fronds. The delicate flowers are arranged in small clusters at the ends of wiry stems. All in all, a charming and useful little plant.

How to grow it: This plant can grow well in any soil, and needs only an average amount of water. To keep sweet woodruff looking its best, top dress with compost once a season and shear the spent blooms and old foliage. Hardy in zones 4–9.

How to use it: May wine is a traditional use for this pretty herb. Try making your own version by decanting a bottle of Pinot gris into a container with a handful of crushed sweet woodruff leaves and a few large pieces of lemon zest. Chill and enjoy.

OPPOSITE: When playing with edibles as colorful as brilliant 'Chianti' sunflowers, designing your front yard food garden is pure fun. Photo by Ann Summa.

TARO
Colocasia esculenta

Perennial; large green leaves (sometimes purple-tinged, black, or variegated); rare bloom is an aroid lily-like spear; size varies, up to 8 ft. tall and wide.

Why should gardeners in temperate climates have all the fun? Tropical taro (or elephant ear—the name reflects the shape of the leaves) is as structural and ornamental as a plant can be. The leaves and roots of taro are edible, but even if you if you don't harvest them this plant is a great addition to the garden. Those who garden in hot, humid climates know that other plants will wilt and give up the ghost when things get too heated, but taro just keeps on going. Several varieties are extremely ornamental, with leaves suffused with purple, or tall, violet stems. Plant taro for its majesty and lush drama.

How to grow it: Those big leaves take a lot of nutrients, so grow taro in soil that is full of organic compost and keep it very moist. If grown in sun, it will need extra water; this plant thrives in tropical wetlands, so don't worry if it's a little boggy. In drier areas, grow taro in containers so extra water can be easily provided. Hardy in zones 8–11.

How to use it: In Hawaii, wetland taros are cultivated—the large roots are made into *poi* and the leaves are used to wrap meats for steaming. In other parts of the tropics, the side tubers of the plants are removed and used as a starchy potato substitute. The young taro leaves are often cooked like spinach, but they need to be cooked very well because of the oxalic acid they contain. Another preparation is frying the root into taro chips—easy to make and delicious.

TEA
Camellia sinensis

Evergreen shrub; shiny green leaves; white flowers; upright and open habit; fall bloom; 6 ft. tall × 4 ft. wide.

This is not herbal tea—it's the real thing. Green or black, tea comes from the same plant, *Camellia sinensis*. This pretty, old-world, flowering shrub has high gloss leaves and pristine white flowers that contain a powder-puff of stamens in the middle. Its late fall bloom, at a time when fresh white flowers are hard to find, lends a stately charm to your front yard. This shrub can be a little slow growing, but patience will reward you with an elegant evergreen shrub that you can enjoy in your garden and in your teacup.

How to grow it: Tea loves water and grows best in slightly humid climates. It will flourish with acidic soil and sufficient moisture. Since you are growing this shrub for its young leaves, don't hold back on the nitrogen. Fertilize with well-rotted manure and you'll have plenty of new tea leaves to harvest. Hardy in zones 7–10.

How to use it: For green tea: harvest the young leaves and buds, let them wilt, blanch them in boiling water, then dry them in the oven at a low temperature until all moisture has evaporated. Store in an airtight container and brew as desired. The process for black tea is a little different. After letting the leaves wilt, you must bruise them (use a mortar and pestle or rolling pin), and leave them to oxidize for at least five hours before drying them. Store, use, and be stimulated by the caffeine and the knowledge that you made tea from scratch.

OPPOSITE, TOP: Moonshine yarrow's flat top of clear yellow flowers and silvery gray leaves make themselves right at home in edible gardens. Photo by Ann Summa

OPPOSITE, BOTTOM: Sweet woodruff makes a lovely emerald green carpet in shady spots where edibles might not grow. Photo by Ivette Soler

YARROW

Achillea millefolium

....

Perennial; gray-green to silver leaves; flat-topped flowers range in color from yellow to red to white; spreading habit with sturdy upright flowers; late summer to early fall bloom; 2 ft. tall and wide.

....

Yarrow, an old medicinal herb, is a particularly good choice for an edible front yard. Its small, fernlike leaves are a beautiful lawn substitute, and its flat-topped flowers look wonderful mixed in with the subtle blooms of the edible garden. Choose from scores of flower colors—mix or match yarrow with colorful herbs and do the traditional flower garden one better because you can graze.

How to grow it: As undemanding as a plant can be—sow the seeds and watch them grow. You'll have lovely foliage from the first season, and in the second you'll get the flowering umbels. Go easy on the fertilizer; too much nutrition makes them floppy. Hardy in zones 3–10.

How to use it: Yarrow is a soothing herb with anti-inflammatory properties. Make a compress for sunburns by boiling yarrow leaves, stems, and flowers, and then refrigerating the resulting liquid. You can use this same liquid as a toner for oily skin—soak a cotton ball in it and apply after washing your face.

YUCCA

Yucca species

....

Perennial; long, pointy, lance-shaped leaves; gray to white flowers on tall bloomspikes; spherically arranged sharp leaves on a trunked plant; early summer bloom.

....

Try not to stab yourself getting to the edible flowers of this desert beauty. They are so prized by some cultures that neighborhoods where yuccas line the streets are targeted for harvest as soon as the flowers bloom. If you decide not to partake in the collecting and cooking of your yucca blossoms, you can still enjoy its spherical, star-shaped form as an important structural element. Who wouldn't love a gorgeous, horticultural pincushion in their front yard edible garden?

How to grow it: Give yuccas well-drained soil and a place in the sun and they will give you their glory. If you want a sharp, architectural plant in your front yard but you live in colder zones, *Yucca filamentosa* is for you—it is hardy to zone 5. The colder the climate, the better the drainage needs to be. To improve drainage, add crushed rock to the soil and make sure the plant sits a little high in its hole so it doesn't settle beneath the soil line. Hardy in zones 6–10.

How to use it: Steam or fry the flowers. Or just enjoy the added dimension that yucca gives your planting.

....

OPPOSITE: *Yucca rostrata* in my front yard, with an 'Old Gold' juniper in the foreground. Photo by Ivette Soler

four
DESIGN PRIMER AND GARDEN PLANNER

I am an unabashed plant maniac. When I design, everything is in service of the plantings and the enjoyment of those plantings. I create relationships between plants based on color, shape, texture, mood, and how the plants in question grow together. The result is a complex planting scheme that engages us on many different levels: the visual, the tactile, and the emotional. Successful gardens grab us by the heart, and there is no reason an edible garden can't do the same thing.

Why *not* make our edible gardens extra pretty by applying the same techniques garden designers use to make fancy gardens look great? Smart, decisive plant combination takes the kitchen garden beyond a utilitarian planting of food crops. It becomes an edible landscape. Don't be afraid to think of your edibles as pure ornament when designing your planting beds. The architectural value of artichokes and rhubarb are clear, but don't stop there. Take a look at other edibles with a fresh eye: the vertical stalks of corn draw the eye up and give drama to your garden (or if you live in a more tropical zone, why not try sugarcane?). Think of vegetables as flowers—they will be ripening on the vine and adding interest to your garden for as long as most flowers would. In my front yard I have a 'Sungold' tomato that uses a blue pole cactus as a trellis. The little golden globes ripening next to the cool, spiny tower makes me as happy as any flower would. Happier, maybe, because I get to enjoy their sweet sunny taste as well as their visual appeal.

This chapter gives an overview of the basic design principles—structure, repetition, form, texture, and color—before diving into a few specific elements of edible front yard design, such as herbal groundcovers and traditional companion planting.

the importance of structure

Structure can be built into a garden through hardscape that gives strength and focus. But by using the right plants in the same purposeful way, you give the softscape of your edible garden a backbone. Most of our edibles will be planted, bloom, set fruit, and the remains composted all in one season. It is the planted structure that keeps your front yard looking well put together for the entire year.

Planted structure refers to plants that shine in a landscape from season to season. Their strong shapes, interesting foliage, and endurance give the eye something to hold onto when other plants with more fleeting lives are waning. Structural plants are often dramatic architectural accents but quieter plants can also be used in structural ways (by repeating them in clumps or ribboning them through the landscape). The important factor is their ability to command interest in the garden throughout the seasons, whether as a standout diva or a supporting player.

In areas of the country that put their gardens to sleep for the winter, paying special attention to planted struc-ture adds an extra layer of stability to an edible garden and extends its seasonal appeal. Even when the sky is gray and the ground is fallow and covered with snow, your edible front yard must always have something going on.

....

PREVIOUS PAGE: Creating eye-catching plant combinations with edibles is all about following the same rules that apply to designing with ornamentals. Photo by Ann Summa

OPPOSITE, TOP: Treat your edibles, such as artichokes, just like you would ornamental plants when designing a front yard food garden. Design and photo by Laura Livengood Schaub

OPPOSITE, BOTTOM LEFT: Ornamentally planted borders give the front garden visual interest and a sense of lushness while the edibles are starting out for the season. Photo by Ann Summa. Garden design by Chris Saleeba of Fresh Digs

OPPOSITE, BOTTOM RIGHT: Cardoons are the tall, rangy cousins of the artichoke, and they have as much architectural appeal. Photo by Ivette Soler

NEXT PAGE: A small espaliered apple tree is nestled in this colorful border. Photo by Ann Summa

TEN STRUCTURAL PLANTS

1. *Acanthus mollis* (bear's britches). The large, deeply cut leaves, and 3 ft. flower spikes of this classic plant are frequently used to create structure in dappled shade. (The deep green leaves will be scorched in strong sun). It has a long season in zones 7–11, retiring only in the hottest days of late summer. Once cut back, the leaves quickly return to hold center stage.

2. *Acer palmatum* (Japanese maples). These elegant, deciduous trees for all seasons can't be beat. The foliage unfurls brightly in spring, summer brings fresh, palm-shaped leaves, the fall color is glorious, and interesting branching patterns stand out against a winter sky.

3. *Colocasia esculenta* (taro). In tropical gardens, this plant bestows specimen and structure in one fell swoop. Repeat throughout your garden to direct the eye, or mass them in one area to create a visual full-stop.

4. *Cotinus coggygria* 'Purple Robe' (smoke tree). Just one of these glorious trees can anchor a space and provide a grounding point for the rest of the garden. The velvety purple foliage glows as it emerges, followed by puffy panicles of tiny flowers—hence the common name. The season ends with a bang of orange fall leaves but the pale branches still hold court while bare during the winter months.

5. *Grevillea* 'Robyn Gordon'. This Australian import is a doozy: deeply incised, evergreen leaves, and flowers that look like a toothbrush and a shrimp had a baby. Use this shrub where you want attention—it will draw it there and keep it there.

6. *Juniperus scopulorum* 'Gray Gleam'. This upright juniper grows slowly to its eventual 15 × 5 ft. size. It is a slender silver and gray column that can be repeated for an elegant, formal, stabilizing effect.

7. *Miscanthus* spp. Choose any miscanthus that works in your area and you'll have proof that a plant needn't be stiff and evergreen to provide effective structure. The strength of these grasses is obvious in the growing season but their winter interest is also very appreciated.

8. *Nandina domestica* 'Compacta'. Not all plants need to be drama queens in order to be structural powerhouses. The small shrub's bright foliage that flushes red with the onset of fall, distinctive crimson berries, and graceful form make it a perfect structural player.

9. *Phormium* spp. Another group of plants that will give you countless choices for structural elements. You won't want to use just one—repeat a single variety or mix and match—their power is in the broad evergreen leaves.

10. *Yucca* spp. It's a little easy being evergreen, but yuccas don't take their perpetual presence for granted. They remain sharp and distinctly focal throughout the seasons. This is plant architecture of the highest order.

BORDERS AND BEDS

Borders and beds are the places your garden can run free, and where you can delight in the sheer pleasure of plants and the interesting combinations they can make. Sweeps of related plants in thoughtful combinations express the delight we take in gardening and the passion we have for our gardens. Thinking in terms of borders and beds can be a helpful way to turn your vision into a garden design.

A border is a long, in-ground planting that is part of a boundary of some sort. It defines either the edges of an outdoor space or helps divide large spaces with drifts of plants. Often, the border is viewed from one side, and is arranged with taller plants in the back, medium-sized plants in the middle, and small plants and groundcovers in the front.

In smaller gardens, borders are often up against a fence or a bank of trees but they can also be the boundaries themselves when planted between one yard and another. Well-placed borders of trees, shrubs, and perennials will enhance the appeal of your garden while creating a zone of privacy that can be important when growing food in a semi-public space.

A bed is a smaller planted area, often used as an accent. Beds can float in the middle of spaces, like islands, and be viewed from all sides. Arrange plants by putting the largest plants in the middle and staggering down in height all around the bed. Raised beds are often built to make growing edibles easier, and are accessible on all sides for ease of care and harvest.

Structural plants anchor the borders and beds, and then we put together the planting relationships that please us and create either a backdrop for our edible garden, or a friendly home for edibles to be mixed into. Even traditional farm-style rows will benefit from being surrounded by beds and borders of structural plantings that can help keep your garden beautiful when many edibles are out of season.

repetition, repetition, repetition

There is something garden designers are very wary of. It goes against our nature as designers. When we see it, we recoil in horror, even though we are looking at plants, the things we love most. This gardening faux pas goes by different names: crazy quilt, patchwork, or onesies. Whatever you call it, this is the practice of buying and using one of each plant within a single garden setting. Usually, this means that many different plants are deployed in a haphazard fashion, with little thought to the overall look or cohesiveness of the space. The eye sees so many different shapes, colors, and textures crashing up against one another that no sense can be made. Quite a bit of love often goes into these plantings—they can be energetic and enjoyable—but with a little more contemplation, these plant collections can also have focus. The tool that some of the best designers wield is simple and it starts at the nursery. It involves numbers. It is the rule of repetition.

When we repeat plants, we create structure. While structure can come from plants with strong individual forms, it can also come from using one plant with a softer form in larger quantities. You can create either a massing of one plant (such as lavender placed in a group of three or more), or a ribboning of it (lavender threaded throughout the garden so the eye can follow the line of color and texture). Both ways work to bring focus and weight to what could otherwise be an overly pixilated scheme.

Within a front yard landscape, where our eyes are used to seeing swaths of green foundation plantings that are basically identical from house to house, using repetition will help make our edible gardens subtly blend in while simultaneously standing out. A word of caution: don't veer too far into the direction of repetition and create a monoculture. After getting rid of one monoculture (the front lawn), the last thing we want is an entire cornfield or a tomato-only extravaganza. Be thoughtful while designing and your front yard will win praises for its looks and its bounty.

HOW MANY?

Garden designers tend to almost superstitiously avoid even numbers, while threes, fives, sevens, and nines are imbued with some kind of horticultural design magic. Gardeners should be very deliberate when using two of the same plant as it has a powerful effect; this quantity conveys a sense of strength and formality. I often use two matching plants as "sentinels" to highlight a significant change by flanking an entryway, opening, or gateway. The number four tends to be too stable and boring, especially when repeating plants with strong shapes. As for the rest of the numbers—go for it. Six and eight are even numbers that can be repeated over the space of a garden, just try not to just line them up so the arrangement doesn't feel overly rigid.

The urge to test the waters before you jump in with both feet will keep you from making a statement. Don't be tentative: you can just as easily try out three plants as you can one. Repetition is your friend, especially when working within an edible landscape. One basil plant will give you a few leaves for a pasta pomodoro or a margherita pizza, but you can't make pesto with one basil plant. Plant five! Then add another variety to the mix and plant three of an exotic Thai or cinnamon basil. There really aren't any hard and fast rules in the world of repetition, only suggestions. Play—but play with big numbers.

....

OPPOSITE, TOP LEFT: Repetition is crucial for giving cohesion to a variety of plants. This grouping of *Phormium* 'Jack Spratt', lemon thyme, purple sage, and *Kalanchoe thyrsiflora* is repeated along the curve of the sidewalk. Photo by Ann Summa

OPPOSITE, TOP RIGHT: The pomegranate is a perfect specimen plant. In this photo, it is draped in deep glossy foliage and decorated with eye-popping flowers. Later in the season it will display orbs of fruit, and in autumn the leaves will turn bright yellow before falling. Photo by Ivette Soler

OPPOSITE, BOTTOM: Basils and sages are planted in multiples of threes and fives along this gravel path—a garden this eclectic needs the strength of numbers. Photo by Ann Summa

SPECIMENS

At the risk of sounding like a horticultural hypocrite, I must explain the exception to the "no onesies" principle. Using certain special, focal plants to accent an area or to create a visual moment is using a plant as a specimen. To qualify as a specimen, a plant should have enough power to hold the space and attract the eye. In your edible garden, a specimen could be an unusual fruiting tree, like a weeping mulberry or Buddha's hand citron. Likewise, a specimen may be an important non-edible helper, like a giant agave or blowsy *Spiraea ×vanhouttei*—anything that captures your imagination and strikes a dramatic, individual note in the landscape. Too many specimens make a garden look chaotic, but none at all can be a missed opportunity. Often it is that one special moment in a garden that transforms the space from the everyday into the extraordinary.

LET ME REPEAT MYSELF

Certain edibles are natural repeaters. Corn, for instance, needs to be planted in groups in order to pollinate properly—the tassel (the male flowering structure) must shed and fall on the silk (the female flowering structure). Without adequate pollination, the corn will "cob" which means it will only produce a few large or misshapen kernels. This works to our advantage when planting edibles in an ornamental way. We can use a grouping of corn plants (ten or more) and repeat that grouping three times. This will become a strong, defined moment in the front yard. Yes, it is corn, but it could easily be clumps of giant miscanthus. Corn has the same verticality, the lovely green color, and the elegantly arching leaves that make the large grass so lovely.

While corn needs to be repeated because of the specifics of its pollination, other plants are simply extra social and repeat by sowing and spreading themselves around the garden. I always allow some of my edible flowers, lettuces, and herbs (arugula and chamomile are favorites) to flower and go to seed; then the wind and birds take the seeds for rides to other parts of my garden. Later on in the season, surprise plants turn up in unexpected places. You can take advantage of this promiscuity by transplanting seedlings you find in unwanted places to spots that can benefit from a little rhythmic repetition. However, more often than not, you'll find these "volunteers" in nooks and crevices that could use a bit of fun. Nature is a wonderful gardener, and annual seeds are a perfect way to permit a little freedom and playfulness within your design scheme.

throw caution to the wind: broadcasting seeds

Some seeds can be strewn around the garden and simply watered in; they don't need to be pre-germinated or buried to any depth. These include all lettuces, mizuna, arugula, bachelor's buttons, borage, and a host of others. Simply sprinkling seeds between your existing plants, or *broadcasting*, is a delightful way to add some surprise to your garden. It is easy and fun to throw your seeds to the wind and allow them to come up where they will. But, of course, there are steps to follow for the best results.

Materials

○ Seeds of your choice
○ Sand
○ Water

Steps

1. Prepare the ground. Rough up your composted soil in places you want an easy annual crop, such as lettuce. Lettuce is especially lovely in the front of the border, planted in drifts.

2. Mix the tiny seeds with a tablespoon or two of sand. Adding sand helps space out the seedlings as they are being spread. Even though this is a casual way of planting the seedlings still need to have some breathing room.

3. Sprinkle the mixture of seeds and sand on your prepared soil. The sand also helps identify where you've already seeded so you don't over-seed by mistake.

4. Water the seeds in gently with a watering can or a hose attachment that has a light shower setting.

OPPOSITE, TOP LEFT: Garden writer and urban homesteader Theresa Loe is tickled as she inspects her corn. Corn needs to be planted thickly to ensure proper pollination, which makes it a natural repeater. Photo by Ann Summa

OPPOSITE, TOP RIGHT: Lettuce seeds are easily collected and broadcasted. Photo by Ivette Soler

OPPOSITE, BOTTOM: This powdery wig is a collection of seeds attached to the blooming head of a burgundy lettuce. If you allow a favored variety to bloom and set seed, you may never have to buy it again. Photo by Ivette Soler

form in the garden

The outline of a plant, its silhouette, is the form. When designing a garden it's important to be able to identify the forms of your edibles as well as those of the trees, shrubs, and perennials that will round out your front yard.

FORM

Arching. A fountain-shaped silhouette; these plants start out narrow at the bottom, then widen at the top and "spill." Phormiums, daylilies, chives, and most grasses have an arching form.

Mounding. Many plants display this round, shrubby, billowing form, and are approximately as wide as they are tall. Sages, lavenders, St. John's wort, and roses are all mounding.

Prostrate or scandent. Flat, mat-forming plants, such as thyme, oregano, groundcover junipers, and sweet woodruff, spread out horizontally and are wider than they are tall.

Vertical. These upright plants have a tall and slender outline. Examples would be columnar junipers (such as *Juniperus scopulorum* 'Skyrocket'), pole cactus, and corn.

Vining. Plants with lax stems that need supplemental support are considered to have vining forms, even if they don't twist and twine. Melons are vining, as are peas, beans, passionflowers, and when indeterminate, tomatoes.

Every garden needs a variety of plants with diverse silhouettes to keep it interesting. Vertical forms are always arresting; they connect the lower levels of the garden to the tree layer and carry the eyes upward. But a garden containing only vertical elements—think of desert gardens full of upright cactus in a sea of pebbles—will look stark. Furthermore, arching and mounding plants make our gardens lush by conveying a sense of fullness and density, but unless you have that variation of form the garden can lack distinction.

The varying forms of plants can also help one another perform better ornamentally. The classic example is lavender and roses. Roses have skinny, somewhat ungainly lower stems, but lavender is just the right size and shape to cover up the rose's bony ankles with its billowing mound. Some edibles have skinny ankles as well. Artichokes, for instance, lose their lower leaves as the season progresses—a mound of marjoram would help conceal those naked stems.

playing with texture

If the form of a plant is its general outline, the texture is the size, shape, and tactile qualities of the leaves, bark, and flowers that are inside that outline. Texture is key to successful and dynamic plant combinations, and the smart use of it can turn a good garden into a great one.

TEXTURE

Fine. Fine-textured plants, such as juniper, rosemary, and box, have tiny, often needle-like leaves.

Medium. Most of the leafy plants in edible gardens, like pelargoniums, sages, beans, and chili peppers, are a medium texture.

Large or coarse. This texture is associated with plants that have thicker leaves. Rhubarb, artichokes, and corn are examples.

Rubbery. Often overlooked in edible gardens, large, rubbery textures are valuable when thinking ornamentally. Inherently dramatic, they can be tropical plants like bananas and taro, or dry plants like aloes and agaves.

Grassy. Grassy plants are essential when injecting a garden with textural variation. The leaves capture the breeze like nothing else, tickling neighboring plants and activating the space. Grassy edibles such as chives, lemongrass, and fennel are textural powerhouses.

Like form, one always wants to work with multiple textures within a planting scheme. If every leaf is too similar in size and shape, a planting can look mushy or indistinct. Too many fine-textured plants can start to look fuzzy. And too much big, brassy foliage can lack subtlety. An issue particular to edible gardens is that many plants that provide us with food are of a similar medium leafy texture. Contrasting textures brings balance and excitement to a garden.

....

OPPOSITE, TOP LEFT: The wide, prominent leaves of corn have a coarse texture, which allows it to stand apart from the finely textured plants behind it. Photo by Ann Summa

OPPOSITE, TOP RIGHT: The smooth, sharp, rubbery agave leaves contrast with the other textures in the garden. Photo by Ann Summa

OPPOSITE, BOTTOM: The flowering mound of a rose is glorious, and edible to boot. Photo by Ivette Soler

Texture also affects the way light is reflected in the garden. Plants with large, glossy leaves are more reflective and stand out, whereas plants with fine, needle-like leaves can absorb light and appear more static. Play around and see how these issues of leaf shape, surface, and light change the look of your front yard. Every choice that brings more variety into our edible plantings helps to transition them into gardens that steal the show from that former king out front: the lawn.

EXCITING TEXTURAL COMBOS

- 'Imperial Star' artichoke, 'Apple Tart' daylily, mizuna, nasturtiums
- Lemongrass, catmint, 'Siam Queen' basil, coconut thyme
- Corn, bronze fennel, leeks, marjoram
- 'Berggarten' sage, red shiso, golden feverfew

TOUCH ME

Texture isn't always visual—don't forget the tactile, our sense of touch. Gardening requires us to touch our plants all the time so we should take the opportunity to imbue our gardens with as much sensual pleasure as possible: the smooth flesh of tomatoes and eggplant, the nubby flowers of chamomile, the grassy coolness of chives. Salvias and peppermint-scented pelargoniums are so soft to the touch that they almost invite petting; once you stroke these plants your fingers will retain the lingering scent of the garden. Gardeners are sensualists at heart. Bask in it.

it's a colorful world

Almost nothing makes people happier than color. This holds especially true in gardens where we stand in awe of the saturated, rich, triumphant colors of flowers, foliage, bark, and berries. This attraction is biological: when we swoon over a gorgeous flower, we are being caught up in the mating dance between plants and their pollinators.

I like to consider foliage color first when combining plants for visual interest. Don't think of leaves as the ugly stepsisters of flowers. They are no less enticing, especially these days, when plant growers and hybridizers are feeding our desire for more interesting foliage. Since the majority of the leaves in any garden (but especially an edible one) will most likely be green, it's important to bring other colors to the table in a big way. When you are designing, make certain that your edible garden will have enough color in its leaves alone to make any flower garden jealous. Choose colorful sages and basils, chard with multihued stems, red mustard, 'Bull's Blood' beets, and start playing with the kind of zeal you had when you were a child opening a new box of crayons.

What colors do you just love together? Purple and red? Beautiful. Just imagine how fantastic red chard would look next to a swath of purple sage. Throw in a little zest with 'Mahogany' nasturtium and you have an electric combination that will satisfy your red and purple desires. See? That wasn't so hard. But maybe you want more. Lucky for you there are so many reds and purples in the edible palette that you can create countless combinations. Try Japanese eggplant planted next to red shiso, then add something bright—like golden oregano whose vivid leaves verge on yellow—to contrast with the dusky eggplant and the ruddy herb. Any ornamental garden would be proud to have that vibrant threesome in its ranks.

Once you are happy playing with foliage color, bring the flowers and vegetables to the party. Echo the red foliage in the red chard and purple sage combination with a red vegetable—maybe a dramatic 'Thai Red Dragon' pepper? Then go a little taller and add some deep crimson sunflowers to the mix. When you start thinking of the associations you can make with your favorite colors, playing designer in the garden is pure fun.

EXCITING COLORFUL COMBOS

- Red chard, orange bell peppers, purple sage, lemon variegated thyme
- Scarlet runner beans, 'Green Globe' artichokes, 'Purple Ruffles' basil, silver thyme
- 'Chianti' sunflowers, 'Sungold' tomatoes, 'Red Rubin' basil, golden oregano

OPPOSITE: A squash vine curls up to a "green roof" succulent planting. Variety of texture and color really spice up the garden. Photo by Ann Summa. Garden of Theresa Loe

SEASONAL CONSTRAINTS

Sometimes the combinations you want to make don't quite go together seasonally. In the chard-pepper-sage-thyme grouping, for example, the chard will want to bolt (go to seed) when the weather gets hot, but hot weather is essential for peppers to start setting fruit. Keeping your chard harvested will encourage fresh leaves to continue growing. It will maintain its position in your garden (and on your plate), and give you the pleasure of seeing the combination you planned coexist in your garden. If your chard gives up the ghost, replace it with a more seasonal companion, like red-leaved basil. These are changes we make in our edible gardens anyway, it just takes a little extra thought to incorporate the ornamental aspects of your plantings into their seasonality.

MONOCHROMATIC

Not all gardens need to scream: some can whisper, or speak in a clear, quiet way. I am a fan of high contrast, but I also love the monochromatic garden—the elegantly edited, serene, specific use of colors within the same range. Many people have seen images of the White Garden at Sissinghurst, in England, or have been lucky enough to see it in person. This world-renowned, monochromatic garden plays exclusively with the paler end of the spectrum: cream, white, and bone-colored flowers, and leaves in every shade of gray. It is truly breathtaking.

Holding onto the edible thought, we can further the ornamental appeal of the front yard through focused use of color. A monochromatic edible garden will be a little more difficult because our palette is limited to start with, but why not begin by embracing the first color that comes to mind—green! Doing a meditation on the freshest color, the color that means gardens, nature, and the growing spirit of ecological awareness is a wonderful place to start playing with a simple color range. Think about using yard-long beans and 'Neopolitano' basil, jalapeno peppers and marjoram, zucchini and 'Black Seeded Simpson' lettuce, cutting celery and white-flowered alliums. Bring in select ornamentals that catch your eye and reinforce the fresh, cool scheme, like *Nicotiana alata* 'Lime Green' and whimsical *Asparagus densiflorus* 'Meyersii'. Maybe you'd like to use box hedge as an organizing principle. A formal edible front yard garden celebrating all shades of green would be spectacular.

The monochromatic principles can be applied to all colors. A theme of purple leaves and flowers could create a beautifully moody vibe in your edible garden.

Or let brightness and light reign supreme by spotlighting variegation and chartreuse and golden leaves. If done well, a monochromatic garden can be just as interesting as one that uses the full-spectrum of colors.

EXCITING MONOCHROMATIC COMBOS

- Yard-long beans, flowering tobacco, marjoram, lime thyme
- Yellow-stemmed chard, lemon basil, lemon variegated thyme
- 'Violetta di Firenze' eggplant, garlic, chives, cinnamon basil

BE YOUR OWN COLOR GURU

Some very learned people will tell you all about the color wheel and complementary colors and contrast and hots and cools and tones and hue. That's all wonderful; color theory is important, but this isn't rocket science or brain surgery. We are opening our box of crayons and finding out what *we* like to put together, what looks good to *our* eye. Who cares if the arbiters of color say that orange and pink don't go together? If you have a desire to see your orange bell peppers tickled by the pinky-purple powder puffs of chive flowers, then go for it. In fact, go further and bring in an ornamental orange accent, like *Tagetes lucida*, and carpet the ground with a pink-flowering Mother-of-Thyme. For an extra ornamental feat, throw in *Sedum nussbaumerianum*, a succulent whose rubbery leaves (a glowing orange when grown in full sun) add a strong foliar echo to all those fantastic flower colors.

....

OPPOSITE, TOP LEFT: It is said we eat with our eyes first—feast on these purple-podded beans alongside an Italian red pepper and dainty Johnny jump-ups. Photo by Ann Summa

OPPOSITE, TOP RIGHT: Hot orange nasturtiums seem to taunt the cool, aloof blue flowers of rosemary. Photo by Ann Summa

OPPOSITE, BOTTOM: A monochromatic planting doesn't have to be soft—try playing with the darker leaved herbs. Photo by Ivette Soler

herbal magic

Herbs are the easiest of all edibles to integrate into a landscape. Many varieties of basil, sage, thyme, and oregano have such visual appeal that they are often used in ornamental gardens on the strength of their looks alone. Purple basils bring a depth of color to a planting that is hard to rival. *Salvia officinalis* 'Icterina' is one of the most attractive of all variegated plants, and *S. officinalis* 'Tricolor', with its splashes of purple, white, and pink, is as eye-catching as they come. Use herbs liberally in your edible landscape, the same way you would a gorgeous non-edible. A large sweep of sage can easily stand in for an ornamental front-of-the-border plant, such as lamb's ears, but has the bonus of being handy in the kitchen as well. Even if you live in a colder climate that necessitates potting up your herbs and bringing them inside, or replanting every spring, they will give you a long season of beauty and usefulness.

groundcovers in the edible garden

The groundcover layer is crucial: low plants that knit themselves together are what truly make a garden a *garden*. It's possible to create a vibrant garden out of only groundcovers, but if you have only large plants—disconnected and aloof in exposed soil—all you have is a plant collection. Even if you lay down a mulch layer, the exuberance and detail one wants from a garden just isn't there. But your edible garden groundcovers, herbal and ornamental, will creep, crawl, and carpet their way into your heart by putting the finishing touch on your front yard.

OPPOSITE, TOP: This herbal grouping shows that foliage color and contrast are important considerations when creating an edible garden that can give any ornamental garden a run for its money. Photo by Ann Summa

OPPOSITE, BOTTOM: A horticulturally savvy cat approves of how well this happily blooming carpet of thyme integrates with puffy sea lavender and the dark aeonium. Design and photo by Laura Livengood Schaub

a magic carpet of thyme

Make a patterned carpet in your edible garden by planting different varieties of thyme in contrasting colors, leaf shapes, and growth habits. Consider how the colors mix and mingle in a complex Persian carpet. Then take that spirit into your front yard and have a ball with your thyme.

Materials for an 8 ft. × 8 ft. space

- At least twelve 4-in. pots of the thyme that will act as your base—this would be the main color in a Persian carpet. I love coconut thyme (*Thymus pulegioides* 'Coccineus') for its incredibly flat profile, dark green leaves, and its fast pace of growth.
- At least twelve 4-in. pots of thyme (three or more varieties) that contrast in color and growth habit to your base thyme. If you are using coconut thyme for your base, you could try lemon thyme (*Thymus ×citriodorus*; mid-green leaves rimmed in bright gold, puffy growth habit, and soft pink flowers), woolly thyme (*Thymus pseudolanuginosus*; small, fuzzy, soft gray-green leaves), and creeping red thyme (*Thymus praecox* 'Coccineus'; deep rosy flowers and foliage that turns reddish as the temperature drops in winter).
- Trowel
- Compost

Steps

1. Place your carpet, alternating the thyme varieties to create a pleasing pattern. Space them at least 1 1/2 ft. apart. The nature of these plants is to creep and spread so don't lay them too closely to get instant results.

2. Remember that this is nature and a precise pattern may appear stilted or too formal. Feel free to jazz it up by clustering a few of the same variety together before returning to the pattern.

3. Dig in your thyme one by one, adhering to the design you've set up.

4. Top dress the soil in between your freshly planted thyme with compost. The compost will act as water-conserving mulch and a nutrient-boost to send your carpet off to a flying start.

5. Let it grow. Use it. Enjoy your handiwork.

we go together: edible companions

We have mostly been talking about combining plants for ornamental reasons but traditional companion planting (using the qualities of one plant to benefit another) is another way of associating your edibles that will enhance the design and functionality of your garden. The principles of companion planting that are practiced in classical edible gardens can be applied to our edible/ornamental garden by combining edibles for both beneficial *and* ornamental appeal.

The old garden saying, "if it eats together, it can grow together," turns out to be very true. Tomatoes and basil are classic kitchen companions and they are best friends in the garden as well—basil improves the taste of tomatoes when planted in close proximity. By choosing a colorful basil, maybe 'Purple Ruffles', you take the companion planting idea into the ornamental world. Similarly, planting borage next to your tomatoes is rumored to keep them free of tomato hornworms; at the same time, the contrast of leaf color (gray-green for the borage next to the fresh middle green of most tomatoes) brings some zip to the planting. If you put it all together so those purple basil leaves give depth to the foliage of both the borage and the tomato, you will be using your design eye as well as your green thumb.

Another example of companion planting is the lovely Native American tradition of the "three sisters": corn, beans, and squash. These plants, often eaten together in succotash, thrive as companions in the garden because each provides something for the other to use. Corn is a natural support for the beans to grow on; beans fix nitrogen into the soil, which corn, a heavy feeder, needs; squash shares the soil, preserving moisture, and keeping predators away with its spiny leaves and stems. These plants compliment each other in an ornamental sense as well. The vertical drama of the corn is enhanced by the vining flowers of the beans, and the fullness of the squash plants is a visual plug where the foliage of both beans and corn can be thin. A more ornamental approach could be tri-colored corn, scarlet runner beans, and a variety of round zucchini, such as 'Eight Ball'. That is companion planting firing on all cylinders.

TRADITIONAL EDIBLE COMPANIONS

- Tomatoes and basil
- Peppers and cilantro
- Kale, mint, and onions
- Lettuce, carrots, and radishes
- Eggplants and beans

ORNAMENTAL COMPANIONS

Ornamental plants can also be good friends to your edibles. Perennial euphorbias, for instance, are known as gopher spurge (*Euphorbia lathrys* is the specific gopher spurge but all euphorbias seem to repel these burrowing horrors). Euphorbias can be planted as a companion for the crops gophers love, which is just about everything, but especially artichokes. I wept for my artichokes during a marauding gopher attack that happened when I decided I had too many euphorbias in my front yard and got rid of most of them. A year later, my artichokes are growing in again, thanks to the euphorbias I hurriedly replanted. If you live in gopher country, take advantage of this benefit while adding tremendous visual appeal (narrow, evergreen leaves and dome-shaped chartreuse spring flowers) to your garden. Another great-looking friend in the garden, nicotianas (flowering tobacco), help ward off chewing and sucking insects if grown near edibles.

Take the ideas of plant associations and companion planting and create the edible garden you always wanted. Be bold, take risks. Maintaining a strict edibles-only rule doesn't serve us very well. Cultural diversity works in the garden.

....

OPPOSITE, TOP LEFT: An unusual example of one plant assisting another in the garden: the blue pole cactus is strictly ornamental but its sharp spines allow a tomato to creep up and use it as a trellis, as well as keep creatures from grabbing the tempting little globes. Photo by Ann Summa

OPPOSITE, TOP RIGHT: Nasturtiums are helpful companions in an edible garden. Photo by Ann Summa

OPPOSITE, BOTTOM: Chris and Ashley Saleeba in their Seattle, Washington, front yard—a happy, healthy mix of food crops and ornamentals. No horticultural xenophobia here! Photo by Ann Summa. Garden design by Chris Saleeba of Fresh Digs

five

EDIBLE FRONT YARD GARDEN DESIGNS

These garden designs, inspired by three bona fide front yard edible gardens, demonstrate a wide range of styles. **Discover a creative take on planting in traditional rows, a wild and dramatic mix of edibles and drought-tolerant beauties, and a beautifully balanced meeting point of hardscaped and lush. Perhaps one design will beg to be replicated in your own front yard, or maybe you'll find small pieces of inspiration to borrow from all three.**

 rays, not rows

DESIGN INSPIRED BY THE CHICAGO, ILLINOIS, GARDEN OF SHAWNA CORONADO. PHOTO BY SHAWNA CORONADO

Author, spokeswoman, and eco-activist Shawna Coronado is usually trotting around the globe raising awareness about our impact on the planet. But when she's at home in Chicago, Illinois, you'll find her gardening up an edible storm in her front yard. Her whimsical interpretation of the traditional method of row planting adds extra visual appeal without sacrificing the ease of harvest and cultivation. From Shawna's small front patio, the planting rows spread out in a radiating pattern, like the rays of the sun. In this design, you can relax under the branches of fruit trees, enjoy a glass of iced tea, and watch your food grow in a sunny front yard.

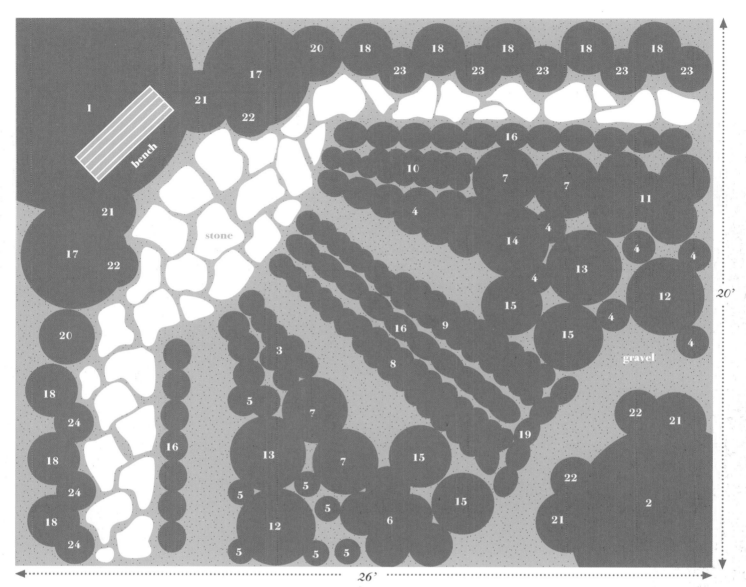

Common name	Scientific name	# of plants
trees		
1 'Firebird' flowering crabapple	*Malus sargentii* 'Firebird'	1
2 'Shiro' Japanese plum	*Prunus salicina* 'Shiro'	1
edible rows		
3 Garlic chives	*Allium tuberosum*	7
4 'African Blue' basil	*Ocimum* 'African Blue'	15
5 Lemon basil	*Ocimum citriodorum*	11
6 'Chioggia Guardsmark' beet	*Beta vulgaris* 'Chioggia Guardsmark'	5
7 'Lacinato' kale	*Brassica oleracea* var. *acephala* 'Lacinato'	4
8 'Lollo Bionde' lettuce	*Lactuca sativa* 'Lollo Bionde'	25
9 'Lollo Rosso' lettuce	*Lactuca sativa* 'Lollo Rosso'	25
10 'Parade' bunching onion	*Allium fistulosum* 'Parade'	14
11 'Bright Lights' chard	*Beta vulgaris* var. *cicla* 'Bright Lights'	5
12 'Black Krim' tomato	*Lycopersicon lycopersicum* 'Black Krim'	2
13 'Copia' tomato	*Lycopersicon lycopersicum* 'Copia'	2
14 'Sungold' tomato	*Lycopersicon lycopersicum* 'Sungold'	1
15 'Eight Ball' zucchini	*Cucurbita pepo* 'Eight Ball'	4

	Scientific name	#
grasses		
16 Blue fescue	*Festuca glauca* 'Elijah Blue'	27
17 'Malepartus' maiden grass	*Miscanthus sinensis* 'Malepartus'	2
18 'Nippon' maiden grass	*Miscanthus sinensis* 'Nippon'	8
herbs		
19 Italian parsley	*Petroselinum crispum*	5
20 Marjoram	*Origanum majorana*	2
21 'Six Hills Giant' catmint	*Nepeta ×faassenii* 'Six Hills Giant'	4
22 Golden variegated sage	*Salvia officinalis* 'Icterina'	4
23 Thyme	*Thymus vulgaris*	5
24 'Aurea' lemon thyme	*Thymus ×citriodorus* 'Aurea'	3

tough and mixed up

DESIGN INSPIRED BY MY INTEGRATED SUCCULENT AND EDIBLE GARDEN IN LOS ANGELES, CALIFORNIA

The act of ripping out my front lawn and replacing it with a drought-tolerant garden was the beginning of my journey to becoming a garden designer. As someone who loves plants, and has grown to love cooking, integrating edibles was a natural evolution. My garden is a designer's laboratory: it's where I play with new ideas, and where I test out color and textural combinations before I use them in clients' gardens. In my borders, vegetables, herbs, and ornamentals happily coexist in close quarters. Basils, sages, and artichokes, chosen as much for color and texture as for taste, cuddle up against large, dramatic succulents. This design is a simplified version of my vivacious front yard; it can be easily installed and maintained, but loses none of the drama and fun.

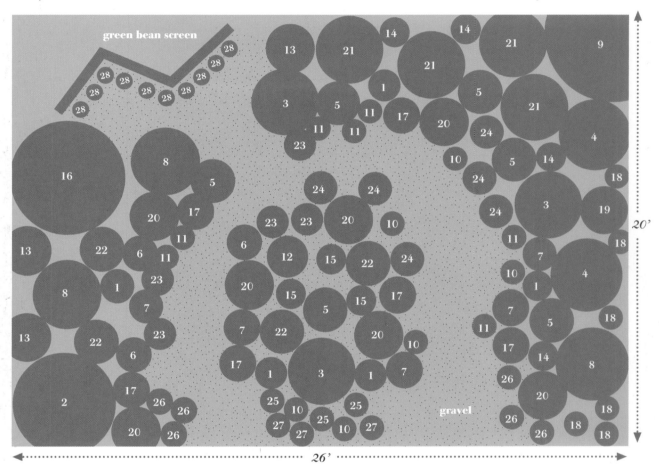

	Common name	Scientific name	# of plants
1	'Zwartkop' aeonium	*Aeonium* 'Zwartkop'	5
2	Variegated Caribbean agave	*Agave angustifolia* 'Marginata'	1
3	White-striped century plant	*Agave americana* 'Mediopicta Alba'	3
4	Weber agave	*Agave weberi*	2
5	'Green Globe' Artichoke	*Cynara scolymus* 'Green Globe'	6
6	'African Blue' basil	*Ocimum basilicum* 'African Blue'	3
7	'Red Rubin' basil	*Ocimum basilicum* 'Red Rubin'	5
8	Mexican lily	*Beschorneria yuccoides*	3
9	Smoke tree	*Cotinus coggygria*	1
10	'Afterglow' echeveria	*Echeveria* 'Afterglow'	6
11	Fleabane	*Erigeron karvinskianus*	7
12	Candelabra tree	*Euphorbia ingens*	1
13	Mediterranean spurge	*Euphorbia wulfenii*	3
14	Bulbing fennel	*Foeniculum vulgare*	4
15	Bronze fennel	*Foeniculum vulgare* 'Purpureum'	3

	Common name	Scientific name	# of plants
16	Variegated false agave	*Furcraea selloa* var. *marginata*	1
17	Ruby grass	*Melinis nerviglumis*	6
18	Mexican feather grass	*Nassella tenuissima*	6
19	'Chocolate Mint' scented geranium	*Pelargonium tomentosum* 'Chocolate Mint'	1
20	'Jack Spratt' New Zealand flax	*Phormium tenax* 'Jack Spratt'	7
21	'Iceberg' rose	*Rosa* 'Iceberg'	4
22	'Mystic Spires Blue' sage	*Salvia* 'Mystic Spires Blue'	4
23	Purple sage	*Salvia officinalis* 'Purpurascens'	5
24	'Tricolor' sage	*Salvia officinalis* 'Tricolor'	6
25	Lime thyme	*Thymus ×citriodorus* 'Lime'	3
26	Variegated lemon thyme	*Thymus ×citriodorus* 'Variegata'	6
27	Coconut thyme	*Thymus pulegioides* 'Coccineus'	3
28	Yard-long beans	*Vigna sinensis*	10

cozy beds

DESIGN INSPIRED BY THE LOS ANGELES, CALIFORNIA, GARDEN OF YVETTE ROMAN AND FRED DAVIS. PHOTO BY ANN SUMMA

Photographer Yvette Roman and graphic designer Fred Davis created a front yard edible garden that perfectly reflects their modern, forward-looking sensibilities. The clean, graphic beds are spare and straightforward; the thick, chunky wood gives each bed's low profile a solid, grounded quality. And in true modern fashion, nothing went to waste in this garden's construction—even leftover fencing material was fashioned into clever tomato cages with an industrial feel. The edges of the two beds facing one another double as benches. Add a few throw pillows and some tea lights, and you are ready for a summer cocktail party in your front yard. To keep food and beauty flourishing year-round, utilize the winter/spring planting list for one of the beds.

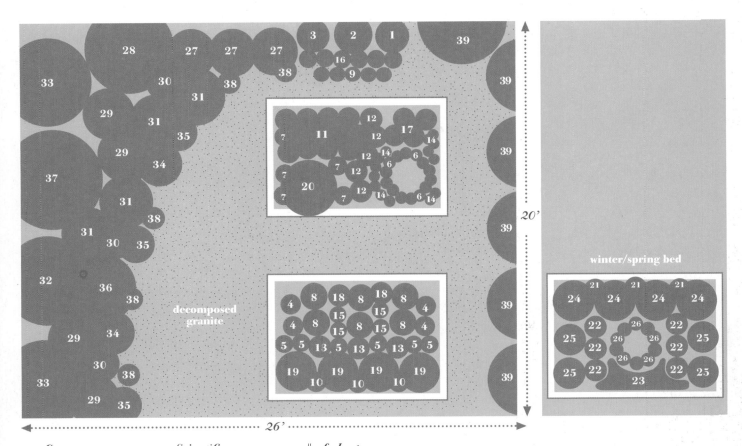

Common name	Scientific name	# of plants
arbor		
1 Armenian cucumber	*Cucumis sativa* 'Armenian'	1
2 Purpleleaf grape	*Vitis vinifera* 'Purpurea'	1
3 'Zucchino Rampicante' squash	*Cucurbita moschata* 'Zucchino Rampicante'	1
beds and under arbor		
4 'Genovese' basil	*Ocimum basilicum* 'Genovese'	4
5 'Pesto Perpetuo' basil	*Ocimum basilicum* 'Pesto Perpetuo'	6
6 'Purple Pod Pole' bean	*Phaseolus vulgaris* 'Purple Pod Pole'	14
7 Borage	*Borago officinalis*	5
8 'Bull's Blood' beet	*Beta vulgaris* 'Bull's Blood'	6
9 Chives	*Allium schoenoprasum*	5
10 Cilantro	*Coriandrum sativum*	3
11 'Silver Queen' corn	*Zea mays* 'Silver Queen'	12
12 'Japanese Long' eggplant	*Solanum melongena* 'Japanese Long'	5
13 Bulbing fennel	*Foeniculum vulgare*	3
14 'Red Sails' lettuce	*Lactuca sativa* 'Red Sails'	14
15 Italian parsley	*Petroselinum crispum* var. *neapolitanum*	4
16 'Orange Bell' pepper	*Capsicum annuum* 'Orange Bell'	6
17 'Chianti' sunflower	*Helianthus annuus* 'Chianti'	4
18 French thyme	*Thymus vulgaris* 'Provencal'	2
19 'San Marzano' tomato	*Lycopersicon lycopersicum* 'San Marzano'	4
20 'White Wonder' watermelon	*Citrullus lanatus* 'White Wonder'	1
winter/spring bed (inset)		
21 Arugula	*Eruca sativa*	3
22 Broccoli raab	*Brassica ruvo*	6
23 'Atomic Red' carrots	*Daucus carota* var. *sativus* 'Atomic Red'	2*

Common name	Scientific name	# of plants
24 'Aquadulce' fava beans	*Vicia faba* 'Aquadulce'	4
25 'Red Russian' kale	*Brassica oleracea* var. *acephala* 'Red Russian'	4
26 'Mammoth Melting Sugar' snow pea	*Pisum sativum* var. *macrocarpon* 'Mammoth Melting Sugar'	10
ornamental border		
27 'Harmony' kangaroo paw	*Anigozanthos* 'Harmony'	3
28 'Purple Pride' Geraldton waxflower	*Chamelaucium uncinatum* 'Purple Pride'	1
29 'Imperial Star' artichoke	*Cynara scolymus* 'Imperial Star'	4
30 'Siskiyou Pink' gaura	*Gaura lindheimeri* 'Siskiyou Pink'	3
31 'Goodwin Creek Grey' lavender	*Lavandula* 'Goodwin Creek Grey'	4
32 Lion's tail	*Leonotis leonurus*	1
33 'Bronze' New Zealand flax	*Phormium tenax* 'Bronze'	2
34 'Chocolate Mint' scented geranium	*Pelargonium tomentosum* 'Chocolate Mint'	2
35 'Berggarten' sage	*Salvia officinalis* 'Berggarten'	3
36 'Winifred Gilman' Cleveland sage	*Salvia clevelandii* 'Winifred Gilman'	1
37 'Limelight' Mexican sage	*Salvia mexicana* 'Limelight'	1
38 Lime thyme	*Thymus ×citriodorus* 'Lime'	5
espaliered on fence		
39 'Anna' apple tree	*Malus ×domestica* 'Anna'	6

* seed packets

six

REALITY CHECK

assess your front yard

I hope you are fired up and eager to start turning your dream of a fantastic front yard edible garden into a reality. **Before the digging and heavy lifting commence, make certain that you understand your front yard by going outside and taking a hard look at what you have.**

climate considerations

Gardening successfully hinges on choosing plants that are appropriate to the general climate of your region, as well as the specific areas of your yard that are cooler, hotter, shadier, or sunnier—the microclimates. Because of the way your house was built, or due to the presence or lack of trees, certain areas may be slightly different than the surrounding space. Utilize these areas of your yard to place your edibles to their best advantage. If you live in a hotter climate, for example, extend the growing period of cool-season crops like lettuces, carrots, peas, broccoli, and kale by planting them under the dappled shade of a tree, or in a cooler, protected area. Try planting edibles that are tender in your zone against a sunny wall, you may be able to successfully grow something you never thought you could. Microclimates are your friends. Find these areas in your front yard and get to know them before you start designing your garden.

Ever-increasing conditions of extreme weather, such as drought and violent storms, are something else to consider during the planning phase. In areas given to long periods of heat and drought, incorporating a tree layer into your design will mitigate the effects of the sun and keep your edibles cooler and not as thirsty. In regions that have been increasingly buffeted by storms and rain, building raised beds in your front yard may ensure that plants get the kind of drainage that helps them flourish rather than drown. These are practical issues, but they are also issues of style. Anything that presents a challenge is an opportunity to incorporate your specific vibe into your garden.

boundaries

Take stock of your property lines. Do you need privacy screening? If so, make notes. Determine whether screening will come from fruit trees, hedges, fences, mesh panels, or a combination. If you live on a corner, be extra aware of maintaining sight lines for passing cars to safely navigate.

Be mindful of your next door neighbors: they can either be your biggest allies or your worst adversaries. If you are on good terms, your neighbors might pitch in on the cost of a blueberry hedge if they get to enjoy the harvest as well. But don't assume they will be delighted that you are growing food in your front yard. Many people have seen examples of front yard farms that they'd rather not have next door. Tell them your plans before you start working. If they have any concerns, address them thoroughly and design your garden to make it work for everyone. If you have to face the glare of a cranky neighbor whenever they pull out of their driveway because your scarlet runner beans are blocking the view of the street, your enjoyment of your garden will be somewhat diminished.

BUDGET TIP: DRAW YOUR PLAN

Before you start buying and building, make yourself a plan. This step helps make certain you have a cohesive strategy for proceeding with the construction of your new edible garden. A plan may sound fairly dispensable for the do-it-yourselfer but it is crucial if you desire to stay on target, on time, and on budget. By drawing your dream garden to scale, you begin to get a sense of what your space will really be. A plan will help you get an accurate count of plants and materials, and more importantly, it will allow you to change your mind without wasting time and money. You'll be able to see problems before they develop and avert potential disasters. For instance, you might notice that you've placed your fig tree too close to an existing arbor. On site, fixing this mistake would require digging, carrying, more disruption of roots—all things you want to avoid. On paper, all you need to do is erase and move it to another location.

PREVIOUS PAGE: Get up close and personal with your yard before you start any construction. Photo by Ann Summa

OPPOSITE: Three panels do double duty as a trellis for growing edibles and a fence to screen out an unwanted view and create privacy. Cucumber vines are starting their race to the top. Photo by Ann Summa. Garden design by Chris Saleeba of Fresh Digs

grading

Some people are lucky enough to have a flat front yard, but others have to create accessible flat spaces where edibles can be grown, tended, and harvested with ease. You will be less likely to interact with your garden if you have to scramble up and down a slope to grab some parsley and chives for dinner. If your yard slopes, find the flattest part of it and site your raised beds there—your ornamental planting borders can gently tumble down the hill, with herbs and artichokes creating an edible division between the two. You may need to bring in someone to regrade the soil to make your space more useable. If your slope is steep and you want retaining walls, this will involve getting permits from the city. Think about these factors and plan as necessary before you begin any planting. Doing things backwards can cost money and time.

existing structures

Are there already built elements in your front yard that you can use? If you have an entryway covered with an arbor, you are blessed with a ready-made place to grow grapes, gourds, or passionfruit. If your front yard is already enclosed with a low wall, use it to espalier apples. Many times we feel like we must have a blank slate in order to design our dream garden, but the act of making something you already have work for you is a fun challenge. How creative can you be?

DIGALERT

Keep in mind that some existing structures—like underground electrical or gas lines—may be hidden, and those are the ones you'll want to avoid. The last thing you want is to accidentally knock out your neighbor's cable internet while digging the foundation for your retaining wall. Take advantage of the free service that exists, in some version, in most counties or cities. Often called DigAlert (or Dig Safely or Underground Service Alert), this service arranges for utility companies to visit sites before digging or excavation happens and flag underground lines and cables, all of which could be costly and potentially hazardous if you dig into them.

light and dark

Look at the sky: where does the sun come from? Does your front yard face the east and get the gentle kiss of morning light? Or does it look west and get the blasting glare of the afternoon sun? For growing edibles, you want as much sun as you can get. Be careful not to add so many fruit trees to your front yard that you create too much shade and impact the successful growth of other vegetables and herbs.

Of course, not every front yard will be sunny and open; your space may be shaded by a tall building or other immovable structure. While most food crops need heat and sun to thrive, some edibles still do well with less light. However, even the edibles that will work in low light conditions will need a few hours of sun throughout the day.

EDIBLES FOR SHADE

- Arugula
- Chard
- Cutting celery
- Hops
- Kale
- Lettuce
- Nasturtium
- Parsley
- Peas
- Rhubarb

OPPOSITE: Especially if you live in hot climates, you can grow food, such as lettuce, in dappled shade. Photo by Ann Summa

tree removal and pruning

Opening up a yard to light can make all the difference in the world to a successful edible garden. If a thick canopy of mature trees (or a cluster of trees placed too close together) casts a dark shade in your yard, consider pruning branches and/or removing trees altogether. Our instincts are to cherish and protect trees, but it may be worth sacrificing a couple of trees to achieve the goal of a productive, beautiful garden space.

Any pruning or removal of trees should be completed by a licensed professional arborist before you begin planting, ideally before you begin any structural work. This way you can see the new pattern of light in your front yard and make any adjustments, such as placing a raised bed in an area that suddenly gets a half day of sun.

Do your research when hiring an arborist: don't let just anybody who hands you a business card touch your valuable trees. Big, beautiful, mature trees can be easily ruined forever by a chain saw wielding know-nothing. Most trees are hacheted so badly that seeing a well-balanced, well-pruned tree is rare—the Holy Grail of garden design. So-called tree trimmers will usually just cut the top off of the tree and trim the end of every branch, resulting in the widespread lollipop look. Our purpose in pruning is to open up the tree to let more light reach the space beneath it. A careless pruning will encourage thick, brittle branches to grow from the end of every cut, resulting in more shade rather than less. Certified arborists will know exactly how to cut the tree you have; they remove entire branches to ensure that careless end cuts won't ruin the inherent shape of the tree. Don't skimp: this is a place where an investment of money really makes sense.

building codes and restrictions

Every do-it-yourself gardener will have to deal with local building codes when constructing a front yard landscape—edible or otherwise. Strict building codes apply to the setback and height of fences and walls, and any terracing done on sloping hillside properties will have to go through the bureaucratic permitting process. In some communities, anything taller than a 4 in. header board used to edge plantings can be considered a wall, and will need either permitting or a variance from the neighborhood council. The same goes for any custom fountains that you build yourself.

Check out the specific restrictions where you live before starting your design process. Horror stories abound, such as homeowners building small raised planter beds getting shut down by a city inspector that just happened to be driving by and asked to see permits for "walls." If you desire, investigate ways to trick the code. In most cases, front fences can only be 3–3 1/2 ft. high but plant material can go higher, and moveable, see-through panels set in the ground to hold vines can be acceptable on the sides of houses (as long as you don't live on a corner lot). A little bit of research before designing will save you money, labor, and heartache later. Understanding what you can't do from the get-go actually opens up your process—you can get creative with the things you *can* do.

the food fighters

A common problem greeted Yvette Roman and Fred Davis when they decided their garden dreams involved growing food: their back yard was deep in shade. The edibles they intended to grow could only be accommodated out front. They began the process of building their garden and quickly ran into a bigger problem—a neighbor who was not on board with a "farm" springing up next door. Thus commenced a battle that ended up before the neighborhood council asking for a variance allowing an arbor between the two yards, and fence to enclose their new front garden. The building codes were strict, but Yvette wouldn't be thwarted. She did research on existing fences and trellislike structures in the surrounding area, the advantages of growing your own food, and the benefits gardens have to the quality of a neighborhood. The rest of the neighborhood rallied around Fred and Yvette, and when the meeting happened, it was full of supporters of their edible front yard. Because of the thought and care that was put into the design of the garden, as well as the support of the community (with one notable exception) the variance was granted and a healthy, productive edible garden now occupies the most prominent position. Kudos to these front yard warriors for fighting the good fight to grow food instead of lawn.

OPPOSITE, TOP LEFT: Most fences in front yards can only be a certain height. Always check local codes before building. Photo by Ann Summa

OPPOSITE, TOP RIGHT: The accordion file represents months of research on the benefits of edible gardening. Photo by Ann Summa

OPPOSITE, BOTTOM: Fred Davis and Yvette Roman had to fight to turn their front yard edible dreams into reality. Photo by Ann Summa

HOMEOWNERS ASSOCIATIONS

Another challenge of suburbia is the often-present Homeowners Associations or HOAs. The restrictions of codes and covenants can hamstring someone who wants to take their front yard and put a more personal spin on it, because the nature of a HOA is to strictly enforce a uniformity of style. Many HOAs demand the front lawn cover a certain percentage of the front yard and be mowed to a certain height.

In planned and gated communities, the desire for uniformity can be a powerful obstacle for the front yard foodie. The fear is of a raucous, unmanaged space that negatively affects property values; the integration of edible plants into a well-designed front yard is a fairly new frontier. But things are changing. With good planning and sound design principles, even a Homeowners Association could be won over by an edible garden.

a plant palette wish list

Make a wish list of all of the plants you want in your front yard edible garden. Look back at chapters 2 and 3 and go to town—pick all the ornamental edibles and helpers that you like. Remember, these lists should serve as jumping-off points, places of inspiration; if you are drawn to other specific plants and they work in your climate, write them down. Creating a wish list is the place to play and dream. Later on, you can narrow down your choices.

When making your palette, remember all of the elements of planting associations: structure, form, texture, and color. These words need to run through your head constantly while making your decisions about plants. Try not to think only about "how much do I *love* this plant?" (although that's a great place to start) but also "how will these plants *work* together?" Have fun, but be thoughtful. Make your list and keep adding to it until it's time to do the actual planting.

....

OPPOSITE, TOP: Beautiful colors and textures come together with good planning. When you make a wish list, think about what plants you want and how they will work together. Photo by Ann Summa. Garden design by Chris Saleeba of Fresh Digs

OPPOSITE, BOTTOM: Some good planning and good advice can help turn your front lawn into an edible oasis, and stand out from the crowd. Photo by Ann Summa

garden coaches

A new kind of garden service is available which gives gardeners the benefit of professional advice and expertise without the commitment of hiring a designer. Before starting your edible front yard project, consider spending a few hours with a garden coach, someone who will look at your site and evaluate its problems and assets. In the long run, getting advice from someone who works with gardens professionally in your area can save you money, time, and heartache.

Pam Penick, a designer and garden coach working in Austin, Texas, helps her clients develop confidence with their gardens and inspires them to make gardening a part of their daily lives. She explains that garden coaches have more of a mentoring role—instructing, enabling, encouraging, and collaborating so clients achieve goals on their own—as compared to garden designers who provide the professional service of designing on paper, and perhaps also installing the garden and offering ongoing maintenance. In tough economic times when everyone is looking for ways to do-it-themselves, garden coaches teach people how to take care of their own landscaping. People have grown comfortable with hiring coaches for other aspects of their busy lives (personal trainers or career coaches, for example) and see a garden coaching session as a way to improve their quality of life by making gardening chores less intimidating.

Garden coaches work with clients in a wide array of situations: someone who wants to learn how to care for a newly installed garden, an experienced gardener who wants to brainstorm with a knowledgeable professional on design ideas or planting suggestions, a home seller seeking advice on adding curb appeal, or a new homeowner who needs help identifying and maintaining existing plants. Find a local garden coach by contacting your county extension service or searching online for "garden coaches" in your city or state.

don't forget
what you have

Now that you have some inspiration for integrating ornamentals and edibles, you'll want to look around your
front yard. A young garden needs plants. Take stock
of what you already have and see how it fits with the
palette of plants you've developed.

Think about how existing plants might work in new associations—they may give unexpected interest and depth
to your design. Take the fortnight lily (*Dietes iridioides*)
for example. Some will turn their noses up at this widely
planted flower for not being exciting enough, but the
advantages of this plant are numerous. It has strappy
leaves and white blooms that look like big butterflies
on wiry stems. It is also a tough evergreen that performs
beautifully in the shade. You may have dappled areas
under trees that you can utilize for lettuces and tender
greens; if those areas are also planted with something
structural, like that fortnight lily, the space may appear
more finished and well thought-out.

So please don't toss a useful and flourishing plant
because you want to start with a clean slate—reuse what
you can. (Instructions for transplanting and potting up
your existing plants are in chapter 7.) Even if you don't
think you like it, save it. A saved plant will always come
in handy. It might even grow on you.

....

OPPOSITE: Many communities have standards that require front
lawns—but you can still grow food along the borders. This cheerful
cottage garden has strawberries, beets, nasturtiums, and even a
small espaliered apple tree. Photo by Ann Summa. Garden of
Theresa Loe

seven

OUT WITH THE OLD
remove and reuse lawn, plants, and materials

So. Out with the old. Not only with the old lawn but with the old idea that we need to have lawn in our front yards. **We know that one of the reasons the front yard is such a perfect place to grow edibles is that it usually has the right amount of sun. So why grow useless lawn? Not only is it entirely unproductive, it is a chemical cesspool—a green carpet that has been doused with herbicide, synthetic fertilizer, and probably pesticides as well. Some people will say "but where will the kids play?" However, most parents don't actually want their children playing in a front yard that's a just a ball toss away from passing cars. Your new front yard will produce something valuable in return for the resources you are putting into it, and will also be a lush living space where you can tend your edibles while gettiny to know your neighborhood.**

If you've already removed your lawn, then you are far ahead of the game. You already know that a planted space is more rewarding than the typical front yard lawn-scape. Creating designs and adding edibles into your existing space is just the latest step in your gardening adventure.

If you feel ready to go big and rip out your entire front lawn—I salute you. If you have decided to do it in stages, I still tip my hat to you. Minimizing your front lawn is a great first step to getting rid of it entirely. I guarantee that after the first year of growing a front yard edible garden, you will start chipping away at the rest of your lawn. It just tends to happen that way—giving water to lawn when you could be giving it to food or water-wise ornamental plantings will seem wasteful. Tending a lawn is nowhere near as rewarding as a garden and simply isn't very fun.

Ready to get started with the rough and tumble business of turning your front yard into your newly designed edible garden? Put on some old scruffy clothes and grab a pair of gloves because you've got a *lot* of work to do—fun work!

....

PREVIOUS PAGE: Follow this sign's advice: for anything but lawn. Photo by Ann Summa

OPPOSITE: Fennel seeds drying on the plant look like sparklers on the 4th of July. Photo by Ivette Soler

get rid of that lawn

Of course, this is easier said than done. One reason turf grasses are the best choice for lawns is that they are tough enough to withstand foot traffic, kids playing, picnics, and other manners of abuse. This "asset" makes lawn difficult to remove—especially organically. Please don't make the mistake of the quick and easy lawn removal strategy of spraying poison over your grass. Yes, it will die. But you will have to deal with the consequences of the chemicals that will persist in your soil.

Sod cutting, solarization, and layering are completely organic, chemical-free ways to begin to eradicate your lawn grass. And when I say begin, I mean exactly that. I don't want to sugar coat this: you'll probably be weeding lawn grass out of your garden beds for years to come. No matter what removal technique you use, seeds and bits of roots will remain in your soil and, if left unchecked, grow into tufts of grass and try to re-colonize your garden. Lawn is an aggressive bully but we can beat it back with time and muscle.

If you choose from one of the excellent methods for organically removing your lawn, your efforts will be rewarded by the knowledge that every bit of food grown will be healthier and more nutritious than anything you could buy in any supermarket. And of course you'll have the pleasure of growing it yourself.

❀ sod cutting ❀

Exactly as it sounds, sod cutting means cutting out your lawn, one strip at a time, with a sharp shovel. Don't go willy-nilly: be methodical and careful. To ensure that no root is left behind, make sure to remove the entire thatch of roots as well as two inches of soil below the thatch. Any piece of root that stays in the soil is a potential spot for re-growth.

Materials

- A tarp
- A sharp shovel
- Some muscle

Steps

1. Lay out a tarp to collect the sod you are going to remove.
2. Use the shovel to cut a line at the far end of the patch of lawn you want to remove.
3. Move over one shovel width, and shovel cut another line parallel to the one you just cut.
4. When you come to the end of the line, turn to face the parallel shovel cuts. Firmly insert the flat side of your shovel under the thatched roots of the sod, and push the shovel forward with pressure from your foot.
5. Begin folding the sod on top of itself three times, then make a perpendicular cut with the shovel.
6. Move the folded stack of sod to the waiting tarp.
7. Repeat until you come to the end of the first row.
8. Repeat steps 2 through 7 until you finish cutting all of your sod.

❀ solarization ❀

Solarization is another organic, chemical-free option for removing unwanted lawn. This method relies on the concentrated heat of the sun to kill the sod, roots and all. It doesn't involve as much sweat, but it takes time, so you have to plan ahead.

Materials

- Water
- Newspaper
- Plastic sheets (enough to cover area)
- Landscape staples
- Compost
- A shovel

Steps

1. Water your lawn well and lay double sheets of newspaper over the area of lawn that you want to remove.
2. Wet the newspaper.
3. Lay the plastic sheets over the newspaper, and secure the plastic sheets with landscape staples.
4. Leave the plastic sheets in place for at least 6 weeks in hot climates, 10 weeks in cooler climates.
5. Once the sod is thoroughly cooked, take off the plastic sheets and use a shovel to flip the dead grass upside down.
6. Cover the upside down sod with 3 in. of compost and then water the area.
7. Replace the plastic sheets and let it cook for another month.
8. Remove the plastic sheets, add a fresh layer of compost, and get ready to plant.

OPPOSITE, TOP LEFT: Muscle and a shovel are the most important tools for sod cutting.

OPPOSITE, TOP RIGHT: Precision shovel work in action.

OPPOSITE, CENTER LEFT: Folding the sod as best you can helps remove it neatly and completely.

OPPOSITE, CENTER RIGHT: Relocate removed sod to your waiting tarp.

OPPOSITE, BOTTOM: A clean, sod-free slate!

Photos by Ivette Soler

LAYERING

Another method, similar to solarization, is layering. This involves smothering your lawn with layers of cardboard and newspaper, and then a thick layer of mulch. Since no plastic is added to trap the heat, this version of lawn removal takes longer than sod cutting or solarization—up to six months. But layering has the advantage of being more presentable, and you can also plant directly into the layers once they have decomposed.

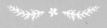

OPPOSITE, TOP: Old brick is in high demand as a landscaping material. If you have some don't get rid of it: reuse it to create a charming walkway. Photo by Ann Summa

OPPOSITE, BOTTOM: Instead of plastic sheets, you can use the layering method to smother sod. It takes longer, but eventually the straw mulch will break down and enrich the soil. Photo by Ann Summa

reusing and repurposing materials

A big benefit of changing an existing space is that you get to reuse the materials that you have on hand to create something new. This is very much in the spirit of the contemporary garden. We want to make responsible choices and nothing is more responsible than recycling. Just because we are saying "out with the old" doesn't mean we have to throw out the old materials. While you are going through your demolition phase, look at what you have and see how you can reuse your material to make it look fresh and interesting, and more appropriate to your new ornamental edible garden.

Let's say you have an old brick walkway that you need to reposition to make room for raised vegetable beds. Save your brick—old bricks are beautiful and can be used to great effect in an edible garden—just change the pattern or mix it up with another material. Maybe you can bring in colored pebbles in between the bricks to change the character of it. Imagine your new mixed brick and colored pebble front walk lined with strawberries or lettuce, or both. If you want to use a different material on your walkway, consider using the bricks you removed to build raised beds, or to edge the borders between your plantings and your paths. Reusing materials is environmentally responsible, and you also save money.

OLD SOD

My favorite use of old sod is as fertilizer since lawn grass is a wonderful source of nitrogenous material. You can create a compost pile of old sod in a sunny corner of your property. To thoroughly compost the aggressive roots and seeds of the sod, you'll need to intensify the heat by covering the removed sod with black plastic. Leave this in place, cooking away, for a few months. Then you can take the broken-down sod and add it to your regular compost pile or worm bins.

You can also repurpose the old sod in your raised beds. Place the sod, upside down, in the bottom of the built beds. Add a layer of compost, another layer of upside down sod, and then fill the rest of the bed with compost. Depending on the height of your raised beds, you can use up a lot of your sod this way. Make sure to put 12–18 in. of fluffy compost on top of the sod.

Your growing garden will welcome the added nutrients from the decomposed sod. Over time, as the sod decomposes and shrinks dramatically in volume, the soil level in the beds will drop. You'll likely need to add more compost to the beds after the first growing season.

Another option is to reuse bits of sod to patch your backyard or other areas of lawn on your property. You can also share it with people you know who have lawn and love it. Donating your sod to maintain their mass of green is a good way to utilize the by-products of building your new garden.

OLD CONCRETE

If your concrete is reusable, it will be hard work, but you can break it up yourself and save the pieces for later projects, such as building raised beds or creating new walkways. Concrete from older houses is generally easy to break up with a jackhammer for irregular slabs or with a concrete saw for more precise cuts. Newer houses, or houses that have had newer concrete work done, might pose more of a problem. If rebar or mesh reinforcement wire was crisscrossed underneath the concrete to stabilize it, it will crumble upon breaking instead of becoming big, rough chunks. If you need to remove concrete (let's say a concrete walkway) and are going to save it, make sure that it is not reinforced. If it is reinforced, you need a jackhammer and strong people to haul away the debris.

No matter how careful you are, you will have small chunks of concrete and gravel that will have to be hauled away. It would be smart to hire a debris removal team to come and take your detritus away—it can be very heavy, hard to load, and expensive to dump on your own. Leave such things to the pros.

removing and reusing plants

Building materials aren't the only things you'll want to reuse. You may have plants in your front yard that, while not edible, will mix well with your new garden. You will want to dig them up, pot them, and hold onto them. Construction is hard on plants so don't leave them in your front yard while building the hardscape infrastructure. Designate a shady area on your property as your plant holding zone. Keep all of your saved plants close together so they can be watered easily and often.

removing concrete

This project explains how to remove a concrete walkway that has not been reinforced. Before you start, designate a convenient holding area where you can store the broken concrete until you are ready to reuse it.

Materials

- Crowbar
- One 4-by-4 piece of wood
- Sledgehammer
- Wheelbarrow

Steps

1. Start at one end of the walkway and dig under the concrete with your crowbar. Pry up a section of the walkway.

2. Insert one end of the 4-by-4 under the walkway and, using the wood as a lever, lift up as much as you can.

3. Hit the slab with the sledgehammer. It should break easily.

4. Place the pieces of concrete in the wheelbarrow and continue this process until the walkway is demolished. Whenever the wheelbarrow is full, take the concrete slabs to the designated space.

OPPOSITE: Fred Davis built cages out of the same material he used on his front yard fence to keep these luscious 'San Marzano' tomatoes in bounds and looking lovely. Photo by Ann Summa

saving trees and large shrubs

It's important to be realistic when saving trees. The chances of a giant tree surviving are very low and anything over 10 ft. tall will be difficult to easily pot up. Young trees have the best chance of being transplanted well.

Materials

- 15-gal. plastic containers (you can get these at home improvement stores or ask local nurseries for cast-offs)
- Potting soil (a commercial potting mix is fine)
- Shovel
- Large pruners

Steps

1. Identify the tree or shrub you want to save and prepare the container by putting potting soil in the bottom.

2. Prune the top branches of the tree or shrub. In the process of digging the plant out you will be getting rid of a large amount of the root structure; help the roots not to have to work so hard by removing at least a third of the branching structure.

3. Cut a circle around the base with the shovel, at least 1 1/2 ft. away from the trunk.

4. Get a feel for the roots and dig down. The idea is to keep as much of the rootball (the roots and the soil that surrounds the roots) intact as possible. You will have to use your pruners to cut through the large roots that hold the tree in place.

5. Carefully dig around the rootball. Estimate the overall size of the rootball—it needs to fit into your container. When you get to the point where you can get your shovel underneath the rootball, make sure you have your container close by.

6. Lift out the tree or shrub, taking care to keep as much soil around the main roots as you can. Place it in the container so it sits tall.

7. Add more potting mix around the rootball, tamping it well to ensure against airpockets. Top off the container with potting soil, but make sure you don't cover the crown (where the tree meets the soil line). Covering the crown can cause stress: it needs to have the same soil level in the pot as it had when it was growing in the ground.

8. Move your potted tree or shrub to your holding zone, and water it every day for a week, and then only when the top 2 in. of the soil is dry until you replant it.

OPPOSITE, BOTTOM: Reuse your sod to make the edibles in your raised beds flourish. Photo by Ivette Soler

potting up perennials and small shrubs

The process for potting up smaller plants isn't as arduous as for trees, but the idea is the same. Give your transplants a good temporary home while they are waiting for the garden to be made.

Materials

- Assorted plastic pots
- Shovel
- Trowel
- Potting soil
- Pruners

Steps

1. Identify the plants you want to save, and make sure you have the appropriate amount of containers.

2. Prepare your containers by placing potting soil in the bottom. Remember, your plants must sit high in the containers, so some will need more potting soil in the bottom than others. Depending on the size of the roots, you can adjust the soil level accordingly.

3. Dig out your plants using the same technique as for the trees. You want to remove as much of the rootball as possible for a successful transplant.

4. Place the plants into their containers and fill with soil.

5. Move your newly potted plants into their holding area and water well.

OPPOSITE: Removing unwanted plants makes room in your garden for edibles you just can't live without, like artichokes. Photo by Ann Summa

unwanted plants

You may not want to keep all of the existing plants in your front yard but don't simply throw them away. The edible garden is a green garden—reuse and recycle as much as you can. Here are a few options for the plants that you won't be integrating into your new front yard.

GIVE-AWAYS

You can put up signs at local community gardens or nurseries letting people know that you have free plants for the taking if they come and dig them out. Set a date and time—maybe two hours on a Saturday. You will be surprised at the power of a free offer. Even if you don't want those plants, they might be just the thing for another gardener.

DONATE

Call your city Parks and Recreation office and see if they will take a donation of plants. They are usually happy to send someone out to dig up and take good, healthy plants. It saves the city precious funds and keeps local parks looking good. Many schools will also take plant donations, especially elementary schools with outdoor classrooms or gardening curriculum. A few well-placed phone calls could get your front yard clear and ready for planting food.

PLANT SWAPS

If you have friends who garden, host a plant exchange party. Provide refreshments, and plastic pots and transplanting tools so that people can dig out whatever they want. Ask your guests to bring unwanted plants or extra cuttings to swap. It's great fun and works like a charm.

COMPOST

If all else fails, compost. A dead or unwanted plant that is composted never goes to waste, instead it is transformed into nourishment for your edible garden.

eight

BUILDING THE BONES

hardscape, privacy, and irrigation

Hardscape is the built part of our landscape—walls, patios, fences, raised beds, and pathways— **anything that isn't a plant. You'll need to put some significant thought into your hardscape in order for your garden to function as a place for edibles to thrive. You may need raised beds to control the soil quality for some of the heaviest feeding vegetables. Trellises will make growing vines easy and they will also introduce an exciting vertical element into your landscape. In many neighborhoods, growing edibles in the front yard isn't a popular thing to do. But well thought-out hardscaping will go a long way toward creating a cohesive space that everyone can appreciate. If done well, you could start a positive trend.**

Good hardscape doesn't need to scream "look at me!" Instead, it should support your planting scheme and allow your space to be occupied in a way that works. Front yards should be inviting and stylish but, above all, they need to be functional. A gravel courtyard that is well utilized and gives the homeowner pleasure is better than a pricey stone landing that looks fabulous for the entire two minutes a guest is standing on it waiting to get inside the front door.

The desire to grow food is part of an overall shift in values and rethinking of how we use our outdoor spaces. The materials with which we build the bones of our landscape are crucial to achieve a result that also melds with our desires to be responsible with our budget and our resources. (Do you *really* need the fanciest stone walkway from the sidewalk to the front door?) You can invest a lot of money in this part of the garden by importing stone from across the country, creating poured-in-place concrete walls, or commissioning a custom-designed water feature. Or you can make smart decisions and create a beautiful, well-designed front yard that you can build on your own, for a reasonable amount of money.

under your feet: pathways and patios

The way we get from here to there is important in any garden but in an edible garden we have to think about access in a different way. When harvesting food, accessibility is key. Always plan for wider paths than you think you need—three feet is the minimum. Creating smaller foot paths, such as a few stepping stones to lead you from a main pathway to the canopy of a fruit tree, will help you harvest without trampling your garden.

If you have the room it is wise to plan a small patio— an area where you can place a bench or chairs—in the garden. This open space gives a visual rest to what can be a raucous, energetic experience for the eyes, and a literal rest for the gardener who has been weeding and

watering. A front yard patio can be the place where you sit and watch the world go by.

When selecting materials, try to find the most straightforward solution to your design issue. If you want a courtyard to compliment your Spanish-style bungalow, simple terracotta pavers would be absolutely appropriate; you can pass on the imported Saltillo tile from Mexico. A bluestone walkway would be perfect for your clapboard house in Pennsylvania but not for your adobe in Arizona. Keep the focus of your garden on the beauty of its plantings, not on the pedigree of the patio.

CONCRETE PAVERS

Concrete pavers are relatively inexpensive, come in a range of sizes, and create a clean, geometric look that fits well with contemporary home styles. The size of the paver is an important consideration: larger pavers lend themselves to a more modern aesthetic while smaller pavers look right at home just about anywhere. You can dye concrete pavers using products found at your local hardware store or online. Staining concrete is simple and effective, and is a nice way to customize your hardscape.

A popular look involves setting pavers a little further apart and filling the joints with groundcovers. (Creeping thymes are especially suited for the edible garden.) This technique is also fantastic with flagstone and urbanite.

PREVIOUS PAGE: A garden like this doesn't just "grow." Smart hardscape lays the groundwork for a well-designed edible front yard. Photo by Ann Summa. Garden design by Chris Saleeba of Fresh Digs

OPPOSITE, TOP LEFT: A young, colorful lettuce nestled among its edible cohorts. Photo by Ivette Soler

OPPOSITE, TOP RIGHT: Thoughtful hardscape makes harvesting easier: this stone path continues through the decomposed granite into the wide, low bed. Photo by Ann Summa

OPPOSITE, BOTTOM: Auxiliary paths should be convenient and unobtrusive. Only a few stones are required to get around this pomegranate tree and to the side of the house. Photo by Ivette Soler

simple concrete paver installation

If you want a small patio or path that is chic, simple, and affordable, you really can't go wrong with precast concrete pavers. They are readily accessible and easy to install with a little help from a partner or friend. It's interesting to contrast hardscape and planting style: a graphic grid can be a perfect counterpoint to a jumble of herbs and edible groundcovers.

Materials

- String
- Stakes
- Shovel
- Bow rake
- Hand tamper
- Crushed granite
- Sand
- One length of 2-by-4 (as long as the width of your path or patio)
- Level
- Concrete pavers
- Broom

Steps

1. With string and stakes, mark out the area of your future pathway or patio to be paved.

2. Take your shovel and excavate the area to 6 in. plus the thickness of your pavers (if your pavers are 2 in. thick, then you should dig 8 in. down).

3. Using your bow rake, smooth out the excavated area, breaking any clumps. When the area is even, take your hand tamper and firmly compact the soil.

4. Lay 3 in. of crushed granite. Even out your surface by adding more granite to dips and less granite to places where the soil bumps up. Wet the area, then tamp your granite to get it as compact as possible.

5. Lay 3 in. of sand. Then you'll need to begin the process of *screeding*—making the sand layer level and even—so the pavers sit correctly. First, firmly tamp your soil. Then, drag your screeding board (a 2-by-4 that is as long as your space is wide) along the surface of the tamped sand; check with your level to make certain things are even. If you are laying a patio, you can screed in smaller sections—just don't step on the prepared sand after you've leveled it.

6. Lay your pavers. Use your 2-by-4 screeding board as a spacing guide to keep each paver in alignment. The 2 in. space between each paver is perfect for filling with decorative gravel or creeping thyme. As you lay your pavers, keep checking your spacing and alignment by putting the 2 in. width of the board in between the pavers at the spaces where the pavers cross—if the 2-by-4 fits tightly on all sides between the pavers, you will have even spacing and straight lines.

7. Check the level on top of the pavers. The pavers should sit level with the surrounding grade. If you need to make small adjustments you can gently lift the pavers and add small amounts of sand to bring them up to level.

8. Once all the pavers are in place, use a broom to sweep sand into the joints, water the pavers to settle the sand, and repeat the process. You will have to do this a few times to get the sand firmly in between the pavers.

OPPOSITE: Concrete pavers are clean, modern, and simple—baby Lola loves her parents' choice of such a chic, economical material. Photo by Ann Summa. Garden design by Chris Saleeba of Fresh Digs

DECOMPOSED GRANITE (DG)

Decomposed granite, a finely ground rock that looks like sand, is a permeable material that allows water to naturally infiltrate the entire garden. Lavenders and herbs look right at home edging a path made of DG—it has the warm, rustic appeal often associated with Mediterranean-style gardens.

DG can be laid loose and tamped with water to a firm consistency, but in high-traffic areas a stabilizer is usually applied to lessen any sloughing off and tracking to indoor areas. It's best to use DG further away from the house so your feet come into contact with harder surfaces that can "clean" any bits of DG off your shoes. For example, if you have a DG patio surrounding a firepit or fountain a little distance from the house, you might want a semi-permeable pathway to your house (perhaps broken concrete dry laid on a DG base) which leads to a concrete landing at your door. By following the progression from softer to harder surfaces in your design, the bottoms of shoes get cleaned off before entering the house. It might seem small or picky but good design is paying attention to details like this. Nobody wants to find that they've tracked hardscape material all over their living room after harvesting their basil.

GRAVEL

Gravel is a wonderful material for pathways and patios, and can even be used as mulch around your plants. Inexpensive and adaptable—there's a size and color to fit any style, mood, or whim—it should not be overlooked as a serious choice for hardscaping.

Gravel sits loosely on top of compacted soil and sand and helps water filter into the earth to feed the roots of our edibles and ornamentals. Herbs love the drainage that gravel provides and the open network of stones are perfect places for seeds to fall into and germinate—you will find more rogue seedlings volunteering in your gravel pathways than anywhere else. In a garden with permeable paving (of which gravel is the best example), it isn't only our planting beds that are alive. The entire space is an active system that behaves in a more natural, symbiotic way than outdoor spaces where walkways and patios are designed to mimic interior flooring. Gravel may not give you the super slick, hard surface that furniture rests easily on inside, but why should it?

OPPOSITE, TOP: Gravel can be rustic or modern, and is an economical option for your path and patio options. Large quantities can be had for a song. Photo by Ivette Soler

OPPOSITE, BOTTOM: Inexpensive pea gravel makes a perfectly appropriate pathway material for succulents and herbs. Photo by Ann Summa

STONE

Stone is a natural complement to any landscape, edible or ornamental, and is a great choice for our integrated garden. It always brings elegance to the landscape, whether used as paving, to build walls, or as a sculptural feature to give weight and balance to a planting. To create a clean, formal look, you can use stone cut into squares and laid without joints, or you can use irregular flagstone for a more casual feel. Either way, be aware that using stone creates a demand for a resource that has to be quarried; it will be removed from the earth with no way to replenish the supply. Stone should be used wisely, sparingly, and always quarried locally and responsibly.

OPPOSITE, TOP: The stone used for this path in Austin, Texas, was locally quarried and therefore more affordable. Photo by Ivette Soler

OPPOSITE, BOTTOM: Urbanite is another name for recycled concrete, the favorite hardscape material in green circles, like the ones photographer Ann Summa runs in. Photo by Ann Summa

URBANITE

A newly discovered raw material called *urbanite* is taking the gardening world by storm. What is it? It is simply recycled broken concrete. This is definitely not the poor, ugly stepchild of hardscape—it can be stained and laid like stone. Urbanite looks fantastic in modern, eclectic gardens packed with edibles. And it fits perfectly into the new paradigm of green living that encompasses all who have sustainable and edible gardens.

If you have concrete to break up, consider yourself lucky. But even if you don't have any concrete of your own (or if yours is reinforced and unusable), you still have options. Recycled concrete is usually available to anyone who can haul it away from construction sites. You can also look for concrete recyclers in your area. Craigslist is a wonderful resource—dumping old concrete (or any removed paving material) can cost hundreds of dollars, so homeowners often list the remnants of demolitions as free for the taking. If you can't get it for free, you'll be able to get it for pennies compared to what you'd be paying for new concrete pavers or stone.

privacy: fences and screens

Privacy is an essential consideration in a front yard garden. You may want your edible front yard to be open and classically welcoming with curb appeal to spare, but you could also use your front yard as a private or semi-private hang-out spot. Many homes have limited backyard spaces so the front yard may be the best place to create an area to occupy with friends and family. Having outdoor areas where you can sit, relax, chat with neighbors, and also have a measure of privacy, can effectively increase the square footage of your home by giving you more actual living space.

In order to create this social space in your front yard, you will want to pick out the best options for fences and screens. When making these privacy decisions, I urge you not to seal off your garden completely. Most of us live in neighborhoods where our front yards are fairly public, visually shared spaces. This is why gardening out front can be so rewarding—you go public with your passion, you share it with those around you, and you get feedback. Imagine the smile on your face when a passing car honks and the driver shouts "beautiful garden!" while you are puttering around. It *will* happen.

Instead, use fences, screens, and plants to create private moments within your front yard. You can have a private patio, and keep the rest of the yard open. Or, keep only your most desirable edibles safely ensconced behind a small fence, away from the hands of passing garden-shoppers. A small citrus or apple tree can be just the thing to screen an unwanted view, if you place it in exactly the right spot. Thoughtful planning is the key to making your garden work the way you dreamt it would.

Woods and metals are the standard building materials for fences and screens. The ones I'll cover are readily available and convenient for the do-it-yourselfer. I believe you can get a great custom look without exotic hardwoods shipped in from South America or Cor-ten steel that costs an arm and a leg.

WOOD

Redwood is a beautiful and classic choice for fences or screens. It can be painted, stained, or left to age naturally (I love this look), whichever works best with your design scheme. Technically redwood is a softwood, but it is no softie when it comes to the elements: it resists warping, shrinking, decay, and insect damage. Do make sure you select the heartwood rather than the lesser-grade outer sapwood. The heartwood is the strong core of the tree (darker, denser, and dryer) while sapwood is weaker and has more moisture (fungus can easily take hold, and it is more likely to shrink and warp while it ages and dries out). Mixed heartwood/sapwood grades are fine for above-ground components, such as the boards and rails of your fence, but the more durable heartwood makes the strongest fenceposts. On the downside, redwood can be expensive, and although it is reforested, many people believe this is not a good product for a sustainable garden unless it has been recycled.

Cedar has a very high oil content, which makes it an especially good material in areas of high humidity. Like redwood, it is resistant to warping and insects (it's no accident that cedar is the wood of choice for clothes hangers and drawers—the aromatic oils repel insects). Cedar is cost effective, about half as much as redwood in most areas of the country. Though it is not as strong, it makes a good substitute for the pricier wood. Cedar is also more sustainable than redwood since it is a faster growing tree.

....

OPPOSITE: Redwood is the go-to fencing material because of its natural beauty and strength. The Saleebas created lovely offset panels as a barrier to screen an unwanted view, and added wire mesh to create what will be, later in the growing season, a living edible wall. Photo by Ann Summa. Garden design by Chris Saleeba of Fresh Digs

Pressure treated lumber is very cost effective (about half the price of cedar) and is virtually rot-resistant. However, in order to make it such a superior rot and decay resistant wood, chemicals are literally pushed into the wood at a high pressure. It is a good, budget-friendly choice for fenceposts, or as a frame for wire fencing. The chances of chemicals transferring into any vining fruit grown on that fence would be minimal, especially if you seal the wood with stain or paint. Pressure treated lumber cannot be used on any farm that has been organically certified for growing food, so if you want to stick to those standards this is not the choice for you. The true risks associated with using chemically treated wood next to edibles, while said to be minimal, are unknown.

Depending on where you live, there may be other wood alternatives: cypress is popular in the southeast, and black locust is a sturdy wood prevalent throughout the Midwest. When possible, select a wood that is readily available in your area. Remember that trucking supplies in from across the country goes against the green and local spirit of homegrown food.

METAL

I love metal: it's simple, modern, and cost effective. You can build (or have built) open metal fence panels or screens, which you can then use to grow the vine of your choice. This "green wall" would be a beautiful backdrop for any garden. Another reason to choose metal is that you never have to worry about resealing, repainting, or decay.

Chain link has an undeservedly downscale, déclassé reputation but it is a fantastic choice for the edible gardener. This inexpensive, widely available material is easily installed and will work as a barrier and a trellis, all in one. Peas in the spring, beans in the summer, or passionflowers all year long—a chain link fence or screen is a functional place to grow food. Chain link has a long life so you may never have to replace it.

Welded wire (reinforcing wire) is heavy gauge wire that is welded into close rectangles, making it strong and open at the same time. Most often used to reinforce concrete, this is a strong and durable material for a fence or screen. The clean, simple wire has a different profile than chain link but offers the same benefits of privacy and trellis in one. It looks great as it weathers and rusts, managing to appear both modern and rustic at the same time. This wire is available only at construction supply stores.

HYBRIDS

A hybrid fence or screen is a great way to combine the warmth of wood with the practicality and ease of metal. A budget-friendly option uses wood as the posts and frame, and a wide link or mesh for the panels. You can stain the wood, paint it, or let it age naturally.

GROW UP!

No matter what material you choose for your fences or screens, you'll want to take advantage of that vertical space and grow vines. Many vining crops need the support a fence or screen can provide—they are natural best friends. Should you decide to build a solid wood fence for privacy, consider installing mesh or wire on the inside of the panels. Vines that you plant at the base of the fence will twine up the supports. (For the non-twining vines, you can easily attach them to the wires with plant ties.) You'll be able to easily harvest your beans, cucumbers, or tomatoes by just walking up to your fence and picking the lovely ripe ones.

OPPOSITE, TOP: This bitter melon vine is curling its way through chain link fencing, creating a type of green wall. Photo by Ann Summa

OPPOSITE, BOTTOM: A double fence allows for different zones of privacy. Design and photo by Laura Livengood Schaub

tri-fold trellis screen

This moveable screen can be collapsed and stored away at the end of the growing season. Build a couple of these to grow peas, beans, or tomatoes and you'll get vertical food, and a measure of privacy. The finished screen is 6 ft. tall × 9 ft. wide, but as it is always placed slightly folded, it is a bit smaller in the landscape.

Materials

- Twelve 6 ft. long, 1-by-$^3/8$ in. pieces of redwood
- Twelve 3 ft. long, 1-by-$^3/8$ in. pieces of redwood
- One 18 ft. length of wire mesh, cut into three 6 ft. panels
- Four hinges with screws
- Screws to assemble wood frames
- Drill
- Staple gun
- Heavy duty staples
- Twelve $^1/2$ in. metal brackets
- Four 6 ft. lengths of rebar
- Hammer

Steps

1. Roughly assemble the six frames: each consists of two lengths of 6 ft. redwood at the sides and two lengths of 3 ft. redwood at the top and bottoms. Use your drill to make small holes and then screw together the wood.

2. Staple one 6 ft. panel of wire mesh to the back of three of the frames. Staple often to keep the mesh taut.

3. Place the remaining frames on top of the mesh, creating three panels. Each panel is a frame-mesh-frame sandwich.

4. Use the drill to screw the panels together.

5. Designate one panel as the center; the two others will be attached to the sides.

6. Attach the hinges to the sides of the panel. In order for the three panels to fold flat (one on top of the other), one set of two hinges will be facing forward, the other set of two hinges will be facing back.

7. Screw in three metal brackets on each side of the back of the center panel. The first set should be 1 ft. from the bottom of the panel, the second set 2 ft. from the bottom, and the third set 3 ft. from the bottom. (In order for the screen to be fixed in place, it will need rebar to stake it into the ground. The rebar will slide through metal brackets on the back of the screen and into the soil.)

8. Screw in three brackets (spaced in the same manner) on the back left side of the left hand panel. Do the same to the back right side of the right hand panel. The end result is one center panel with two sets of brackets for rebar to slide through, and a set of brackets at either end of the screen.

9. Place your screen in the landscape. Slide the rebar through the brackets and firmly pound them into the ground with the hammer. Your structure should be moveable but secure.

10. Grow something lush and delicious on your finished screen.

OPPOSITE, TOP LEFT: This screen is easy to make and can be moved to suit your needs from season to season. Photo by Ivette Soler

OPPOSITE, TOP RIGHT: The screen becomes clothed in bean foliage, then long beans emerge later in the season. Next season—maybe gourds. Photo by Ivette Soler

planting for privacy

In most cities, codes will not allow tall fences directly in front of a home, but hedges and trees can be grown without restriction.

The crisp lines of a well-trimmed hedge can be a smart contrast to a joyful jumble of edibles, but it is also important not to overdo a good thing. There is something sad and unfriendly about driving through a neighborhood lined with tall front hedges blocking even the tiniest glimpse of the world beyond. A 3–4 ft. hedge allows for a view from the street to your house (and visa versa); place a bench or chairs nearby and once seated you'll never know you are curbside.

Blueberries. If you have acidic soil, a blueberry hedge would be lovely and fun; the only problem would be sharing your harvest with the local bird population. (Bird netting is an easy answer.)

Box. This classic hedge material makes for a neat, fresh (non-edible) element in your front yard edible garden.

Olives. *Olea* 'Little Ollie' is a small non-fruiting olive that grows 4–6 ft. tall and wide. It has lovely deep green-gray leaves and takes very well to shearing. Although it bears no fruit, this stylish hedge is a perfect helper for an edible landscape.

Rosemary. Please don't be jealous if you can't grow rosemary as a hedge—many hot zone dwellers would love to grow blueberries in long sweeps. Rosemary is fragrant, has lovely blue blossoms, and (when the climate is right) can be quickly coaxed into a 3 ft. hedge.

Roses. *Rosa rugosa* or *Rosa glauca* are fantastic flowering, fruiting hedges suitable for a variety of climates. The beauty proffered during the growing season makes up for its bareness in the winter months.

Use fruit trees to gently "baffle" views rather than obliterate them. A front yard orchard is charming and useful, and there are fruiting trees for every climate zone. Always take the mature size of trees into consideration and be careful not to plant so many fruit trees that you risk casting too much shade on your planting beds. Remember, vegetables and herbs will grow better given as much sun as possible.

Apples. Everybody's favorite fruiting tree is incredibly beautiful in leaf, flower, and fruit. Apple trees are especially easy to espalier so you can turn a simple wire fence into an elegant fruiting feature that takes up little space and helps give you a modicum of privacy.

Citrus. In warmer climates you can grow lemons, oranges, kumquats, grapefruits, and even exotic citrons and blood oranges as effective screens. These trees can be planted as multi-trunked specimens, and naturally grow in a shrubby way—leaves from the bottom of the truck to the top.

Fig. The beautiful fig tree is a wonder. Big, bold leaves create an almost tropical effect, and the branches are flexible enough to espalier against a wall or fence.

Plums and Cherries. The delicate flowers of cherry and plum trees are incredibly beautiful harbingers of spring. They can provide gentle screening when underplanted with medium-sized shrubs like lavender and rosemary. By mid-summer, you will be eating ripe, juicy fruit, hidden from view.

Pomegranate. These thickly branched, dramatic shrubs or small trees are perfect for creating nooks. The branches are flexible and take well to shaping.

BUDGET TIP: PRICE IT OUT

Go through every hardscape element and figure out your materials list for each project. If you are building a moveable screen, for instance, you'll need to account for not only the main material (wood) but everything you will need to build the screen (wire mesh, screws, staples, rebar, and fasteners). By doing this for every hardscape element you have included in your design, you will be able to price them out in detail before purchasing anything. Don't forget to include the soil for your raised beds and borders.

OPPOSITE: In some zones, rosemary can be grown as a large, stately hedge, and will add privacy to your yard. Photo by Ivette Soler

raised planting beds

Raised beds are an enormous asset in an edible garden. Gardening in raised beds gives you the opportunity to use the very best soil—either your own compost or purchased planting mixes. No one walks on raised beds so you will have the fluffiest, loveliest soil to work with. It'll take very little work to add more organic amendments to your beds, and your plants will appreciate their rich and aerated home. In raised beds, the soil will also warm up faster (allowing you to plant vegetables earlier in the season) and any weeds that blow in and germinate are easily pulled out.

Since you probably won't want a big labyrinth of raised beds in your front yard, prioritize bed space for the plants that are the heaviest feeders (which includes many favorite vegetables). If you don't have enough room to accommodate the medium feeders in a bed, they can go in the ground in well-amended soil. Light feeders will flourish in unamended soil in the ground.

HEAVY FEEDERS

- Brassicas (cabbage, broccoli, and kale)
- Corn
- Eggplants
- Peppers
- Tomatoes

MEDIUM FEEDERS

- Beans
- Cucumbers
- Greens
- Peas

LIGHT FEEDERS

- Lettuce
- Marjoram
- Oregano
- Sage
- Sunflowers
- Thyme

Raised beds are most commonly made out of stacked concrete or stone, bricks, and wood. All make stylish and functional beds, but it's helpful to do a little research before choosing materials.

STACKED STONE AND RECYCLED CONCRETE BEDS

Both stone and recycled concrete are good material choices for beds—you won't have worry about issues such as decay or chemicals possibly leaching into your food. Recycled concrete is eco-friendly and long lasting. Stacked stone is classically beautiful and an excellent detail for your edible beds. This material will be pricier than other options, but if you source your stone locally you can still get some bang for your buck.

The process to make stacked beds out of recycled concrete or stone is easy, and can be done without the use of mortar. Stack the slabs by moving from layer to layer, staggering them until you've reached your desired height. Because you will be perching on the sides of the beds when you garden, you'll want to put the top layer of stones, the "capstones," in place with a little quick-drying cement, a trowelful at the center of the stone so it won't be seen on the edges. Fill the bottom 4–6 in. of your new raised bed with gravel, and then fill with the compost and soil mix of your choice.

OPPOSITE, TOP LEFT: *Ipoema batatas* 'Marguerite' tumbles out of a raised metal bed. Photo by Ann Summa

OPPOSITE, TOP RIGHT: Creamy, white 'Easter Egg' eggplant is a heavy feeder and does best planted in a raised beds. It makes a fresh black and white combo with the leaves of *Ipomoea batatas* 'Ace of Spades'. Photo by Ann Summa

OPPOSITE, BOTTOM: The stone beds in this side yard, visible from the street, are stately and have a permanence and solidity that is hard to beat. Photo by Ivette Soler

WOODEN BEDS

Gardeners most frequently choose to build their raised beds with wood. The flexibility of design that wood allows is tremendous: create a rustic, homey look, or go to the opposite end of the design spectrum and build spare, clean, modern boxes.

Wood is more vulnerable to the elements than stone, concrete, brick, and other harder building materials. Beds made of thinner cuts of lumber (2-by-6s for example) will need internal supports to help them resist warping and popping. The internal supports can be rebar or strong aluminum piping held to the wood with brackets. Beds constructed with heavier stock (such as 4-by-4s) can typically hold their shape without internal supports.

It is wise to avoid building raised beds with pressure treated lumber. The chemical issues discussed in regard to fences take on a greater urgency in our beds since the wood will be in direct contact with the soil that edibles will grow in. Though studies have shown that only minimal amounts of chemical preservatives actually leach out of the timber into the surrounding soil, when dealing with the food you are feeding your family, prudence is top priority. If pressure treated lumber is what you have on hand (perhaps recycled from another area in your yard) you can create a barrier between the wood and your soil with a polyvinyl chloride (PVC) liner commonly used for ponds.

HYBRIDS

While visiting my hometown of San Antonio, Texas, I spied some fantastic raised beds made of corrugated metal framed by recycled wood. The look was exciting and functional, and conveyed a modern, industrial vibe into the edible garden. Use materials imaginatively when designing your front yard beds. Don't be afraid to be unconventional.

SIZE MATTERS

When designing and building your raised beds, keep practicality in mind. Don't make your beds so big that you can't reach the center from any point. You want to be able to reach in and do your work without having to kneel or step on your fluffy aerated soil. A raised bed shouldn't be any wider than 3–3 1/2 ft. Vegetables should have a free and easy root run, so give them at least 12 in. to stretch and wander. If you go a bit higher (18–20 in.) the gardener will have a nice perch while digging or just enjoying the moment in the garden.

OPPOSITE: Due to its availability and clean good looks, wood is the preferred material choice for raised beds among edible gardeners. Mexican squash (calabacita) dangles, scampers, and crawls, but still looks purposeful and contained in this bed. Photo by Ann Summa

hellstrip beds

The space between the sidewalk and the street is usually a no-man's-land of turfgrass and weeds. This is where people disembark from their cars, where skateboarders fall while practicing tricks, and where people curb their dogs. Known in gardening circles as the hellstrip, this is the hardest place of all to garden.

Sometimes ambitious homeowners will plant the hellstrip and incorporate it into their front yard design. However, if the city needs to access power lines or gas mains and the hellstrip planting interferes, then goodbye garden. Anything planted in the hellstrip needs to be tough and essentially temporary. How do we approach this space as part of our front yard food garden? How do we make something useful and well-designed that can also be taken apart at a moment's notice should the powers that be descend? These were my challenges when I decided to utilize my hellstrip to extend the reach of my front yard edibles.

My hellstrip is in an extremely public place: one block away from a big high school and on the corner of a busy intersection. Protecting my beds from being vandalized and my food from being stolen was a high priority. Time has made me understand that one has to roll with the punches when gardening in public urban spaces. Yes, some people will steal your edibles if they are in this visible space—the ornamentals that I planted around the beds are spiky for a purpose. But on the flipside, other people will be inspired. My neighbors compliment the hellstrip beds when I see them at the market, cars stop and ask me how I built them, teenagers from the high school tell me how "cool" they are. And I am in love with what they give me and how they look.

I planted the area in between the beds with a few agaves and grasses to blend into my front yard's tough backbone, and then covered the ground with a dark gray blend of pebbles.

....

OPPOSITE: Inspired by my Texas roots, I constructed freeform temporary beds out of corrugated galvanized steel. The beds were built in an afternoon and can be easily taken apart. Photo by Ivette Soler

making heaven in hell

I adore the look of the round stocktanks that I've seen many gardeners in Austin, Texas, use as planters and ponds. The hybrid wood and metal beds I saw in San Antonio struck my fancy as well, so I decided to combine the two ideas and create raised beds using simple strips of corrugated metal riveted into circular shapes. The resulting beds are clean, simple, and incredibly useful. They are great-looking homes to corn, zucchini, tomatoes, peppers, eggplant, and a host of herbs and companion plants. The whole process could not have been easier and took just one afternoon to complete.

Materials for one round bed (12 in. tall × 5 ft. wide)

- Eight panels of corrugated metal, cut to size (these panels were 28 in. wide; the width may vary depending on where you buy it)
- Drill
- Rivet gun and rivets
- Eight 20-in. rebar or steel rods
- Wire hardware cloth to line the bottom of beds

Steps

1. Lay out your panels and overlap each by 2 in.

2. Starting at one end, prepare to attach panel to panel by drilling three holes down each seam, evenly spaced through both panels.

3. Using your rivet gun, place a rivet in each of the holes.

4. You will now have one long strip of metal. Take it to the designated location in the hellstrip and stand it up.

5. Rivet the final seam that will turn the strip of metal into a circular bed.

6. Place the support rods on the outside of the beds and pound them into the ground until they are even with the top of the beds.

7. Cut lengths of hardware cloth to fit inside the bed. Place them in the bed so they overlap and curve up the sides.

8. Fill your new bed with compost and start planting.

OPPOSITE, TOP LEFT: Corrugated metal is easily found at home improvement stores, and can be cut to order. Riveting the cuts together is simple and quickly done.

OPPOSITE, TOP RIGHT: Pound in steel rods on the outside of the beds to help the metal keep its shape.

OPPOSITE, CENTER LEFT: Once the riveted beds are placed, install wire hardware cloth at ground level to discourage burrowing rodents.

OPPOSITE, CENTER RIGHT: Fill the beds with compost, bagged or homemade.

OPPOSITE, BOTTOM: One month after planting, corn, chard, tomatoes, and herbs are beginning to flourish in the most public of places.

Photos by Ivette Soler

water water everywhere

The decision of how to irrigate your edibles is exceedingly important. If your system of watering breaks down, for even a few days, all of your hard work could be gone for the season. It can be your biggest expense, so it is not to be taken lightly. Whatever method you choose should be dependable and within your grasp. If you live in Arizona, handwatering your front yard food might not be the best choice. A pricey pop-up automatic irrigation system might be overkill for someone living in Seattle. How you decide to deal with your watering issues can make or break your garden.

HANDWATERING

My time spent handwatering my first garden was when I discovered that I wanted to spend my life gardening. I formed deep relationships with my plants and began to understand how associations work in a garden. I saw insects do damage and watched how other insects could keep those bad guys in check. I became a real gardener because I took the time to go out and water my fairly large collection of plants by hand, every day.

When watering by hand, you have total control of your watering and can quickly respond to the individual needs of plants. You'll learn that some vegetables can't handle water on their leaves, some need a light spray, others need a deep drink, and still others might benefit from a drenching of fish emulsion cocktail.

The downside of handwatering was that I couldn't travel for more than a few days without entrusting my garden to well-meaning but essentially unmotivated waterers. Twice, I came home to devastation. It was heartbreaking. It is rare to find someone else who will be invested enough in the success of your garden to patiently water by hand. If you know someone like that, wonderful: you can have a handwatered garden and a life!

....

OPPOSITE: This nasturtium has captured the evidence of the morning's watering. Handwatering takes time, but it allows you to form a deeper relationship with your garden. Photo by Ann Summa

DRIP SYSTEMS

A drip irrigation kit from your local hardware store works very well for many gardens. These systems are inexpensive, easy to install, and get the job done. You can choose from a variety of watering styles: sweaty soaker hoses, laser-drilled soaker hoses, or flexible pvc with drip emitters (different emitters allow for varying rates of water flow, giving you excellent control over the watering needs of your plants.). You can even set up little mini-misters on risers to direct a soft spray over your tender greens (salad greens really benefit from a nice humidifying spritz in the heat of the summer).

Putting these systems together is actually fun, in a puzzle-like way. Once you've configured your drip kit you can attach it directly to your hose bib and manually turn it on when watering is needed, or use a battery operated controller. Consider going all the way and getting an automatic timer—it's worth the added cost. Simply forgetting to turn on your hose bib for a couple of hot days could result in a shriveled bed of mesclun.

Things to watch out for: the flexible tubing can get clogged and needs frequent flushing. The system can also get damaged by wild animals looking for water, and those bites and holes might not be discovered for days. The misters on risers are easily broken by dogs and children running around the garden.

BUDGET TIP: THE REAL COST OF IRRIGATION

....

Even if you are not sure if you want an automatic, in-ground irrigation system, it's smart to get a bid for a comprehensive system to be installed by professionals. Get three bids from reputable, licensed contractors, and then price out the cost of a do-it-yourself installation of a drip irrigation kit. Factor in your time as well, and the peace of mind you will have knowing that your system is going to give your edibles the best chance to survive and thrive. You need to know the real cost before you can make a decision and finalize your budget.

AUTOMATIC SPRINKLERS

Automatic, in-ground sprinkler systems are a wise investment in the success of your garden. If you decide to incorporate automatic sprinklers into your edible garden, you can be assured that your plants will get the water they need when they need it. You can travel and know that your plants are taken care of, and you won't wake up to discover a loose piece of spaghetti tubing creating a bog under your chili peppers. The rigid pvc pipes are installed by professional contractors, underground, and are connected to sprinkler heads that are flush to the ground and pop up when the system is activated. The sprinkler heads are flexible—you can easily adjust the spray zone from a narrow quarter-inch circle to complete 180 degree coverage.

An important advantage of these systems is that a good, even spray is essential for the knitting together of a creeping groundcover layer. Thymes, for example, have small roots right at the surface of the soil. Only with an even spray does the surface of the soil get moist enough to encourage this connection. Once the soil is covered, the plants themselves keep the soil cool and moist, so you can use less water. Many people think sprinkler systems are only for water wasting lawns and are automatically bad—not so. You can use their power for the good of your front yard food garden.

HYBRIDS

In my design practice, I often set up my clients with a combination of in-ground sprinklers and drip systems. In the integrated edible garden, the combination of drip and pop-ups makes especially good sense. If you have raised beds, drip tubing can direct the water right to the soil and away from leaves that are vulnerable to moisture, such as tomatoes and squash. This could help keep these crops that sometimes have ratty leaves looking good enough to hold their own in the front yard. A good, solid, state-of-the-art in-ground system that incorporates drip lines is the single best investment you can make for your front yard edible garden. If you can afford it, you should do it.

OPPOSITE: Strong lines and shifts in materials form a simple yet powerful framework. The pavers leading from the house to the street, bisected by the public sidewalk, is an especially nice touch. Photo by Ann Summa. Garden design by Chris Saleeba of Fresh Digs

grow it dry

Experts agree that a serious water crisis looms on the horizon. Reservoirs, rivers, and streams are drying up and drought is an ever-present threat in many parts of the country. It is our responsibility to save water when and where we can. Prioritizing the productive growing of food, rather than an ornamental lawn, is a big step in the right direction. However, it's equally important to use water wisely when growing food. Here are some drought-tolerant edibles that can be grown lean and dry.

- Amaranth
- Chives
- Jerusalem artichoke
- Marjoram
- Opuntia
- Oregano
- Pineapple guava
- Pomegranate
- Sage
- Thyme

nine

WORKING IT

organically maintaining
your front yard

Organic food is grown without the use of any synthetic or artificial agents: no herbicides, pesticides, or fertilizers that have any chemical components. **Why does our front yard edible garden need to be strictly organic? The answer is simple—we don't want to put anything into our bodies and our environment that can be harmful to us. All chemical fertilizers, pesticides, and herbicides leave residual traces in our soil and, subsequently, in the crops we grow. If we use these sprays in our edible gardens, the toxic chemicals will eventually be consumed by our families and friends—the very people whose lives we are trying to enhance when we grow our own food. Every choice we make in the garden impacts the world around us, so taking steps to garden with simple, straightforward techniques that eschew chemical fertilizers, herbicides, and pesticides is vital.**

Thankfully, there has been a real shift in our level of awareness and desire for organic food in recent years. But while organic options are now available in most grocery stores, the price of purchased organic food is often prohibitive. Gardening organically, however, is not expensive. You rarely have to even buy anything—most of what you need to be an effective organic edible gardener is probably in your kitchen right now. If we grow as much as we can in our gardens like our grandparents did, we can avoid bad, chemically laden food products.

Organic and sustainable gardening practices take a little more time and effort than the standard methods but the benefits outweigh any inconvenience. Once you get the hang of it, gardening the natural, organic way is easy.

THE BENEFITS OF ORGANIC GARDENING

You are putting life back into the earth.
Pesticides and chemical fertilizers persist in our soils, making it an unfriendly environment for beneficial microbes and other organisms like earthworms which convert decaying organic matter into healthy soil. By using organic methods, your garden becomes literally alive, below ground as well as above.

You are helping to reduce the toxic load in your community. Chemicals used in gardens wash away into storm sewers, and thereby into our rivers and oceans. By gardening organically, you are taking a stand against the polluting of our waterways.

You are protecting upcoming generations.
The impact of toxic farming practices are profound, and affect our children in direct ways. Children are particularly vulnerable to toxins. Decades worth of agricultural chemicals in our food and water supply may have a direct link to increased levels of nervous system disorders, such as autism. Not only will your healthy food and lack of chemicals be positive for your children, your choices affect your community at large.

building healthy soil

The most important thing that you can do for your edible garden is to organically build healthy, rich soil. Soil is the foundation for every success you have in your garden: crop yields will be better, vegetables will be bigger, and herbs will be packed with flavor. The recipe for healthy soil is simple—add compost. And the best compost is the compost you make yourself because then everything that goes into your soil is under your control. If you start ahead of time, you can customize your soil to meet the specific needs of your edibles.

Thought about fertilization has changed over time. The idea previously centered around plant-specific fertilizers: rose food for roses, citrus food for lemon trees, and vegetable food for edibles. All that is, frankly, is a way to sell you something that you don't need to buy. We don't really need to feed our plants if we feed our soil with homemade, organic compost. Making our own compost, allows us to control what goes into it—we know it's organic and we know it's good. Your edibles will be tastier, more nutritious, and you'll know exactly what goes into what you grow, every step of the way.

....

PREVIOUS PAGE, TOP: A gulf fritillary visiting 'Genovese' basil is a common scene in an organic garden. Photo by Ann Summa

PREVIOUS PAGE, BOTTOM: In this lush, beautiful, and healthy garden, the only amendment is compost and the only pesticides are water and the gardener's fingers. Photo by Ann Summa. Garden of Laura Cooper and Nick Taggart

OPPOSITE: Why garden organically? Because all of our choices, positive or negative, impact future generations. Lily's parents have chosen to keep her food free of anything suspicious by growing most of it themselves, using organic methods. Photo by Ann Summa

the beauty in compost

Making compost is easy—you can choose not to make it a chore. We lead busy lives, and not everyone can devote themselves to the tending of an edible garden and a complicated composting situation. I like to remember that compost happens naturally—whether we want it to or not, things are decomposing all around us and adding to the soil layer.

Composting involves combining an equal amount of green matter (lawn clippings and fresh leaves) with brown matter (dead leaves, newspapers, cardboard, or twigs). Many things that are often thrown away can and should be composted.

SAVE IT

- Green matter: grass clippings and garden trimmings
- Brown matter: dead leaves, cardboard, newspaper (not glossy), straw, chipped wood, and ashes
- Kitchen waste: fruit and vegetable peels, any fruit or vegetable past its prime, coffee grinds (even the filters are compostable), teas bags, and egg shells
- Weird stuff: dryer lint, hair from your hairbrush, and the "ick" from your vacuum cleaner

SKIP IT

- Diseased plants: these might infect your new garden
- Oils: a sure way to a slimy compost pile
- Coated, glossy paper, or envelopes with glassine windows
- Human, cat, or dog feces: all are full of bacteria
- Meat and animal fats: these will bring rodents straight to your pile
- Wood chips, sawdust, or ashes that you aren't certain came from untreated lumber
- Napkins and paper towels that have absorbed oils or sneezed-in tissues
- Weeds: don't even take the chance

compost creation

Select a warm, sunny spot to site your compost pile. In order for your compost to properly decompose, it needs to have a tight, warm center. Containing your compost—in a proper bin or just with sides so the compost won't spread out—is ideal. You can buy a composter or you can make your own. You can build a compost bin in as many ways as you can frost a cake, but I always find that simpler is best.

Keep in mind that smaller items (such as shredded paper and chopped up veggie peels) will decompose faster than big, thick leaves and sticks. If you wish, you can help break down any thick leaves by running over them a few times with a reel-type lawnmower.

When adding kitchen scraps to your compost, be certain to bury them in the center of the pile. This will help keep critters away from the good stuff that will become garden gold in a few months. The center of the pile is the hottest, and the decomposition of kitchen scraps will heat it up even more. Turn your pile often if you add kitchen waste to make sure that all parts of your pile get the benefit of that deep, internal heat. The hotter the internal temperature of the pile, the quicker your compost "cooks": a hot compost pile can give you organic amendment in as little as two months.

Carefully monitor the moisture level: a compost heap needs to be kept damp but not wet. This is where things can go awry. Many well-intentioned compost piles turn into smelly, slimy messes because they are too wet; or they stay an inert pile of leaves and twigs and never decompose because they are not wet enough. Create the goldilocks of compost piles—the one that is just right—about the wetness of a well-wrung-out sponge. If you properly site your compost heap in the sunniest available spot, you will probably avoid the wet smelly kind of heap, and a quick sprinkling once or twice a week will give your pile the moisture it needs.

....

OPPOSITE, TOP: You can purchase compost bins or make them yourself from a variety of materials. The one pictured is made out of wood and has removable slats for easy access to compost. Photo by Ann Summa

OPPOSITE, BOTTOM LEFT: A simple compost cage can be quickly made out of inexpensive materials from your local hardware store. Photo by Ivette Soler

OPPOSITE, BOTTOM RIGHT: These wiggly creatures will become a mighty legion of garden minions, consuming kitchen waste and turning it into powerful organic fertilizer for your edibles. Photo by Ivette Soler

Once you have your organic matter contained, gathered, and moistened, you'll want to turn it once a week or so to make sure that all your compost gets cooked. Just get in there with a pitchfork or shovel and let out your aggression on that heap of potential goodness. If the weather is warm, the moisture level is optimal, and you turn it regularly, you can have compost in two to five months.

JUST SAY NO TO MOW AND BLOW

All around the country, the sound of leaf blowers generate a loud undercurrent to our daily lives. The odd thing is, there is no reason to use them. Leaves are supposed to be left around the root zone of trees. A tree is a miraculous organism and one of the most incredible things about a tree is that it feeds itself. As the leaves on a tree get old and fall off, they litter the ground under the canopy and decompose. During decomposition, the leaves become alive with beneficial mold and bacteria; they become nutrition. As they decay, they feed the soil around the tree and we know that what feeds the soil feeds the tree. It is a simple, beautiful system that leaf blowers disrupt. The demand for perfection in our gardens, and the need for lawns free of leaf debris causes an imbalance that then has to be addressed by using synthetic fertilizers. If we just let our leaves sit, we let nature do what it does best.

vermicomposting

Compost takes room. The smallest effective compost pile is 3 ft. × 3 ft. but they are often bigger. If you don't have enough room to accommodate traditional composting, try getting some friends to pitch in. I have thousands of friends that help me compost: earthworms. Composting with worms—vermicomposting—is a fast, efficient, incredibly easy way to use your kitchen scraps and yard waste. The worms work fast digesting scraps and yard waste, and the payoff is a supercharged version of regular compost. This has been called "garden gold," which is basically the nicest possible way you could say "worm manure." It will make all of the edibles you grow robust and delicious. Another bonus to vermicomposting is that it's done in closed bins so you won't have to worry about vermin poking around in your pile. Vermicomposting may be the single best thing you can do for your garden. If you get worms, treat them well. They will be your allies in organically growing the best food you possibly can.

simple compost cage

This is a simple, easy, inexpensive way to enclose your compost. The wire keeps the air circulating around the decomposing material, which helps prevent it from getting damp and smelly.

Materials

- Measuring tape
- Rubber mallet
- Four 5 ft. lengths of 1/2 in. rebar
- One 12 ft. length of fine gauge wire fencing or hardware cloth, at least 3 ft. wide
- One 4 ft. length of medium gauge wire, cut into 4 in. pieces

Steps

1. Find a sunny corner in your backyard or side yard and mark out a 3-by-3 ft. square.

2. Place your rebar posts in the corners and bang them into the ground at least 1 ft. with your rubber mallet.

3. Starting with one post, attach the edge of your hardware cloth with three 4 in. pieces of wire: one piece at the top of the cloth, one at the bottom, and one in the middle.

4. Move to the next post. Bend the hardware cloth around the post at a 45 degree angle and use three wire pieces to attach it at the top, bottom, and middle. Continue to the next post and around the square. Finish by attaching the end of the hardware cloth to the first post.

5. Now you can load it up with green waste, brown matter, kitchen scraps, and even dryer lint.

OPPOSITE: A dense, multi-colored mix of herbs says "cottage" and "homey," but also forms a barrier against weeds. Photo by Ann Summa

in the event of weeds

Weeds in your front yard food garden can't be allowed to gain a foothold. A plant that is weedy can grow so vigorously that it steals nutrients and space from the food crops we are lovingly tending. If left unchecked, weeds will negatively impact the growth of your edibles and the beauty of your design. The specific kind of weeds you have will depend on where you live, but one guarantee is that you *will* have weeds.

I believe that the biggest weed is turfgrass. And unfortunately, no matter how hard you worked to get rid of your lawn, it's inevitable that some of it will come back. It is tough and tenacious and now that you have rich soil to grow edibles in all over your garden, you'll be seeing your erstwhile lawn trying to stage a comeback.

When it comes to gardening organically, elbow grease goes a long way. One of the areas where this is especially true is weed abatement. Getting rid of weeds without herbicides is an important part of your organic edible gardening practice. Here are some tactics to try.

PULLING, RIPPING, AND TUGGING

The old, tried-and-true method of manually digging out weeds might be time consuming, but it is the best way to assure these aggressive thugs will be history. Some weeds are annual and others are perennial with stronger roots (they may also come up at different times of the growing season). Hand weeding should be a regular part of your gardening routine, but thankfully, if you are persistent, weeds become less of an issue over time.

MULCH YOUR HEART OUT

Isn't it great that improving your soil also helps get rid of weeds? A thick layer of compost used as "mulch" creates a physical barrier—the dormant weed seeds can't get sunlight. The ones that *do* germinate will be far easier to pull because the roots have taken hold in light, fluffy soil.

BOILING MAD

Simple boiling water can be an effective weed killer when applied repeatedly. Use a teakettle and pour the boiling water all over the leaves, stems, and root zone of the offending invaders. Be careful not to pour the hot stuff on any of your desired garden plants.

WEAPONIZED VINEGAR

The higher the acidity the better, but even the 5 percent acid concentration of ordinary household vinegar will get rid of weeds if applied more than once. You can heat the vinegar in a teakettle and pour it out, or you can put it in a spray bottle and squirt it on the leaves. Don't worry about it changing the pH level of your soil—vinegar doesn't persist so soil pH will return to normal within a few days.

WHAT NOT TO USE

Burning. There are torches that are sold specifically for killing weeds, but I'd be very careful. This method is literally playing with fire.

Plastic sheet mulch. Pure aesthetics: plastic sheeting used as a permanent mulch is ugly. Even if you cover the sheets with compost or gravel, they will inevitably show through and look awful.

Roundup. This is the most popular herbicide used in the home garden. While rated as the least toxic of all herbicides, it is still disruptive to the environment. The active ingredient, glyphosate, has been found in high levels in rivers and lakes close to agricultural areas.

let them drink tea

Compost tea is an excellent liquid fertilizer for your edibles—and the process for making it is as simple as can be. Scoop 1 cup of compost (regular compost or the wormy kind for an extra kick) into a coffee filter and tie it securely with a piece of twine. Then let the "tea bag" steep in a bucket of water for 24 hours. Decant this nutritious concoction into a spray bottle or watering can and use it to give a supercharged boost to your edibles.

OPPOSITE, TOP: Any weeds that dare to come up in your garden are in real hot water. Photo by Ivette Soler

OPPOSITE, BOTTOM: Snails are raging alcoholics and can't resist beer. Better they drown than snack on your lettuce or golden oregano. Photo by Ivette Soler

organically controlling pests

As organic front yard gardeners, we can't just go get a bottle of poison and kill all insect intruders in one fell swoop. It takes more time and tenacity to do it the responsible way but it's worth it. When it comes to organic critter control, I find myself revisiting a few helpful methods over and over again; I call it my organic arsenal. The key is persistence. Keep an eye on your edibles and apply these organic anti-pest interventions much more frequently than you would with chemical treatments.

YOUR HANDS

When our grandparents saw bugs on food crops, they would pick them off with their hands and drown them in a jar of kerosene. If it was good enough for them, it's good enough for us. I regularly inspect my edibles and pick off worms, beetles, and other creeps though I use a jar of alcohol instead of kerosene.

WATER

Your hose is a valuable weapon in the war against the bad guys who want to eat your tender front yard victuals. A strong jet of water will blast aphids and whiteflies off the leaves of lettuces, kale, and artichokes.

BEER

Beer is a well-known targeted pest control technique that helps eradicate slugs. You can create a slug suicide soup by sinking a pie tin in the ground near any crop that slugs have started to attack and filling it with beer. Slugs are attracted to yeast and will dive in and drown in the beer bath. What a way to go. Set your trap at night and in the morning all you have to do is pick up the container and throw out the disgusting contents.

PEPPER AND GARLIC SPRAY

A classic in the organic gardening arsenal, this spray irritates the flesh of soft-bodied suckers and chewers like aphids and cabbage worms.

making pepper and garlic spray

It's best to make this spray fresh, right before application. Reapply as needed, and after rain. If you have any of the mixture left, store it in a cool, dark place and use it within a week.

Materials

- Blender
- 5 hot peppers such as scotch bonnets, cayennes, or jalapenos (the hotter the better)
- 4–6 cloves of garlic
- 1 cup warm water
- Funnel
- Coffee filter
- Spray bottle
- 3–4 drops Dr. Bronner's dishwashing soap

Steps

1. Place the peppers, garlic, and warm water in the blender and puree. The mixture should be watery but try to blend out all of the chunks. Let the mixture sit for about an hour.

2. Line the funnel with a coffee filter and use it to decant the pepper mixture into the spray bottle.

3. Add 3–4 drops of Dr. Bronner's dishwashing soap to the bottle, then fill it the rest of the way with water.

4. Shake the spray bottle to mix the soap and pepper/garlic water. (Be sure to shake the bottle before each use.)

5. Spray the leaves and stems of your plants and the soil around the root zone.

OPPOSITE, TOP LEFT: Organic ethics are proudly on display. Photo by Ann Summa

OPPOSITE, TOP RIGHT: My sweet little neighbor Ana was the commander of the ladybug release. Photo by Ivette Soler

OPPOSITE, BOTTOM: Purple sage creates a back door for a sprig of marjoram flowers, which are powerfully attractive to bees. Photo by Ann Summa

LADYBUGS

Releasing ladybugs in your garden is not only magical (especially if you have a child helping you), but these charming spotted creatures will work hard keeping aphids at bay. I released ladybugs at the beginning of every growing season for the first four years of my garden, but now they live and breed there all year long. Planting fennel, parsley, yarrow, marjoram, and thyme provides places for these wonderful beneficial insects to lay their eggs.

URINE

Sorry to be crass but urine is a well-respected method to deter some of the larger pests and critters. Fox, coyote, and bobcat urine are commercially available online and in many specialty nurseries. The idea is that small animals will smell the scent of a larger predator in the area, and leave the garden. Apply around the garden and spread terror among the critters trying to grab your edibles.

the two-legged critters

When growing food anywhere in the garden, one always has to anticipate and protect against the multi-legged creatures. In the front yard, an additional varmint may go after your hard-earned crops: other people.

By planting food behind a small hedge or fence, you make it psychologically harder for someone to actually go into your private space and take your edibles. The act of picking becomes less casual and more like vandalism. Often we plant fruiting trees around the edges of the garden; if so, we should accept that much of what hangs over the fence into the sidewalk will be taken by passers-by. It's a small price to pay. Whatever is lost to those with sticky fingers is miniscule in comparison to the fruit your tree will give you for years and years to come.

The temptation to pick fruits and vegetables that are not yours, but are accessible, is somewhat understandable. Walking by a garden bursting with fruits hanging from trees and vegetables getting riper by the day *is* tantalizing. When I moved into my home an enormous avocado tree in the side yard yielded the tastiest avocados—and the neighborhood felt just as entitled to them as I did. Fencing in the side yard gave me control of my crop but I felt badly about denying my new neighbors their free treats. I decided it was only right to share my bounty, and when that tree died of old age, everyone who lived nearby mourned right along with me.

The ethics of sharing are ingrained in gardening: we pass along cuttings, we share seeds, and when we have bumper crops we offer the excess goodness to friends and neighbors. This generosity will help you when you grow food in a visible, fairly public space. Do what comes naturally and share with the people who live around you. Let them know what you are doing and enlist their help in keeping an eye on your garden. In most cases the people walking by your home regularly—neighbors walking their dogs, children going to and from school, mailmen or delivery people—are the ones most likely to pick. The desire to pick can be diminished, however, if you aren't a stranger. Be friendly and gracious. If someone expresses an interest in your gardening, offer to pass on a zucchini when it ripens, or reach down and clip a few sprigs of basil. You will make a friend and an ally, and maybe even prompt another person to grow food out front.

adjusting your expectations

An important part of gardening the organic way is getting used to how edibles and other plants really look. The spotless, perfect gardens in magazines and on television give the home gardener unrealistic expectations. The gardens in front of our houses are not photoshopped, but gardens in magazines often are—chewed leaves or evidence of chlorosis are taken away—and what remains is a garden that doesn't really exist. Organic gardens are beautiful but they are not perfect. Anyone who gardens without chemicals has had to learn to accept a certain amount of raggedy leaves, mildew, and other unavoidable realities. The type-A personality can learn a lot by gardening the organic way because it is virtually impossible to maintain photo-ready standards without chemicals.

Do your best. Build your soil. Plant to attract beneficial insects. Keep a few old-fashioned pest control methods in your back pocket. Most of all, enjoy the fruits (and vegetables) of your labor!

....

OPPOSITE: Somebody has been nibbling on my pepper leaves! Not all of your plants are going to be picture perfect and magazine beautiful. It's okay to let your garden be real—all gardens are. Photo by Ann Summa

ten

HARVEST TIME AND BEYOND

Your edible front yard is flourishing and looking glorious: in late spring, peas are dangling from their vines and lettuces are as frilly as big peonies. In early summer, bright artichokes are plump and red-leaved beets are starting to pop out of the soil. In mid- to late summer peppers are coloring up and the corn is sweet and ready to eat. What are you waiting for? It's time to get in there and harvest that food. But this can be so hard to do. For those who grow ornamental edible gardens, altering our designs by harvesting is an issue infused with ambivalence. We want the edible garden that we designed to shine but we also want to eat the wonderful, tasty stuff we are growing in it.

Be that as it may, we can't forget that the first and foremost reason we grow food is to eat it. Harvesting, preparing, and eating the food we grow is a joy. And a marvelous part of growing edibles from the design perspective is that we get to create different ornamental relationships throughout the growing season—harvesting our crops gives us the space and opportunity to play with other ideas. Take advantage of the short growing season of most food crops and create fun, new planting associations, or expand on the ones that worked in previous seasons.

ready to replace?

Because our curbside gardens are so visible, we want to make the times when we have to harvest entire plants (beets, corn, or fennel, for instance) as easy and seamless on our design as possible. Smart front yard foodies will have replacements—a few containers of annual edibles—ready to swap in for whatever is harvested. The best filler plants are fast growing and will quickly plug any empty spaces so your front yard design stays attractive.

FIVE REPLACEMENTS FOR HARVEST HOLES

1. *Amaranth:* can replace kale, chard, and other cool-season greens in your summer garden.

2. *Arugula:* grows fast starting early spring through late fall in many zones. It can replace both spring and summer plants.

3. *Lettuce:* a good multi-season replacement that fills in well. Looseleaf varieties are especially versatile.

4. *Parsley:* tuck in parsley to fill in holes throughout the growing seasons. For variety, use curly parsley in addition to Italian parsley.

5. *Spinach:* an excellent cool-season replacement for basil, shiso, and other tender herbs.

....

PREVIOUS PAGE: In the summer garden, amaranth is a good replacement for cool-season greens, like spinach. The young leaves also make a seamless spinach substitute in the kitchen. Photo by Ivette Soler. Garden of Philip Leveridge of ESP Design Services

OPPOSITE: Herbs grow fuller and faster if you snip them, so use them regularly. Your cooking will be tastier and your garden will be lush and fragrant. Photo by Ann Summa

snip snip

It's natural to be a little tentative about cutting our precious crops, but food growers must be maniacs with the pruners and snippers. Except for a few plants that have to be harvested in one fell swoop, we can actually eat our edibles and grow them too. In fact, the very best way of maintaining your edibles is to trim and eat them. Just like when one prunes an ornamental plant, when you cut any part off the top of an edible, you are changing the relationship of root to leaf. After cutting, there's more root than leaf so the root system has an easier time creating leafy growth. The buds just below where you cut (or at the crown of the plant, depending on the type of plant) are swelling with hormones and will soon burst forth with fresh, tender stems and leaves.

Harvesting kale, chard, lettuces, and spinach by the handful keeps the plant lush and tender, and you well-fed. And the bonus is your garden stays populated with lovely edibles longer than if you harvested the entire plant at once. I love to thickly sow looseleaf lettuces so I'll have crisp leaves to snip whenever I want. Herbs, like many garden plants, are a classic example of this "use it or lose it" style of harvesting. Basil, shiso, sage, marjoram, oregano, parsley, and rosemary all particularly benefit from being cut—they quickly become better, fuller plants.

Your foray into regular cutting in your garden also leads to fantastic opportunities in the kitchen. If it's time to pinch back your basils, then it's time to make pesto. Have the ingredients ready and whipping up enough for an Italian feast will be a snap. Try using branches of rosemary as a basting brush while grilling or roasting meats. Or if you have a swath of purple sage in your garden, make fried sage leaves as an appetizer for your next dinner party. Your guests will be delighted and your sage will soon be bigger and bushier. Even though our edibles were selected for their ornamental potential, they are still food—destined to be enjoyed on the plate as well as in the garden.

washing up

When gardening in the front yard, your homegrown food is an easy target for some of the more unsavory aspects of urban living. The neighborhood dogs may have a penchant for marking the lemon thyme that edges the sidewalk in front of your home; feral cats can sometimes mistake gravel pathways as litter boxes; and when passing cars spew oily, sooty exhaust, some of it can (and will) land on your veggies. It is important to clean every bit of food from the garden before eating it.

Not using pesticides means that you are going to find little friends curled up in your edibles. This is totally natural, in fact, it is a good sign of your commitment to a healthy family and a healthy planet. Don't be freaked out when a spider crawls out from a crevice on the underside of a leaf of chard—better it happens while washing than sautéing. Run your fingers along the nooks and crannies so that nothing sneaks its way into your salad. Squeamishness is a thing quickly left behind when gardening. We are tough. We are urban pioneers. We can handle a pest or two or ten, and whisk them off our homegrown food without a second thought. But pests also leave residue. Aphids secrete sticky honeydew that attracts dirt and ants, and caterpillars leave droppings (as well as themselves cocooned in a curly leaf edge). All of these potential meal-ruiners need to be spotted and carefully cleaned away before you prepare and eat your bounty.

One of the pleasures of harvest time is simply being outside in your lovely, bountiful yard, enjoying your handiwork. Just look at all that wholesome goodness— go ahead and pat yourself on the back. Sometimes, in the middle of this self-pleasure, it's hard not to eat something right then and there, without cleaning it. If you simply can't resist the temptation to pop a little nugget into your mouth, then give it a little squirt from the hose first. Enjoy. Let your neighbors see you enjoy. Make them a little jealous.

 oust the ick

All of the natural (and unnatural) icky things we don't want to consume can be removed in a few simple steps. The process takes a little time but quickly becomes second nature.

Materials

- Large bowl
- Soft cloth
- Colander
- Apple cider vinegar

Steps

1. When outside harvesting, take a good look at your produce. Inspect it for bugs and give it a good shake to remove any dirt or droppings. Wipe vegetables off with a soft cloth.

2. Designate a large bowl to soak your edibles in. Place it in your sink, fill it with cool water, and swish your produce around for about a minute. When dealing with lettuces, greens, broccoli, or anything with a wrinkled texture where beasties can easily hide, swish it a little longer. Drain by lifting your produce out of the water and placing it in a colander. Empty the bowl and give it a quick rinse to remove sediment.

3. Make a solution of 1 part apple cider vinegar to 4–5 parts water in the bowl and soak your goodies in it for 2 minutes. This diluted apple cider vinegar mixture has been shown to work better than commercial vegetable washes. Give them another few swishes and lift them out into your waiting colander.

4. Give your harvested goods a final quick rinse. Now you are good to go.

OPPOSITE, TOP: After the artichoke flower is spent, the entire plant will be cut down to make way for a fresh flush of leaves. Photo by Ann Summa

OPPOSITE, BOTTOM: Be sure to clean your front yard edibles scrupulously before eating. Interested parties with four legs love to sniff and leave their calling cards. Photo by Ann Summa

can I make it stop?

There is a point in every gardening season when all of your planning and preparation comes to a delightful head. You might even have a bumper crop—an excess of your favorite food—especially if you've followed the design rules of repetition and safety in numbers. All this goodness is great, but when you've had eggplant parmesan, eggplant stirfry, eggplant hummus, eggplant fritters, ratatouille, and enough grilled eggplant to choke a mule—and more eggplant is coming—then what?

Preserving the surplus bounty from your garden allows you to control your diet even when the high seasons of spring and summer are over. It is part of what makes growing food such a valuable endeavor. Preserving your harvest might sound difficult or time consuming, but it doesn't have to be. With a little planning you can easily preserve your favorite goodies from your front yard and enjoy them during fall and winter.

FREEZING

Freezing homegrown food keeps the nutrient levels high and the texture intact. The steps for fruits and vegetables are slightly different but both are simple and done in a flash.

An important thing to note when freezing anything: water is the enemy. Water expands as it freezes, causing the cell walls to rupture and the food to become mushy when prepared. This is why it is crucial not to soak your soon-to-be-frozen edibles, and to make certain they are very dry before freezing. Some fruit, like strawberries, have so much water in them they are best used after freezing for syrups or smoothies. Regardless of preparation, these morsels of summer bounty will surely be appreciated in the middle of winter.

OPPOSITE, TOP: A Japanese eggplant dangles independently among purple basil leaves. Where once there was only one, soon there will many. Photo by Ann Summa

OPPOSITE, BOTTOM: Berries are ideal candidates for freezing—you don't even need to cut them. Photo by Ivette Soler

❧ freezing fruit ❧

Fruit, especially berries, are easy to freeze. The question is: with sugar or without? I prefer the natural and simple route.

Materials

- Fresh fruit of your choice
- Sharp knife
- Towels
- Parchment paper
- Cookie sheet
- Plastic freezer bags
- Plastic straw
- Marker for labeling bags

Steps

1. Prepare the fruit by cutting it into evenly sized pieces and removing any stones or pits. Berries are the perfect size to freeze so leave them intact.

2. Quickly wash the fruit—do not soak it.

3. Thoroughly dry the fruit on towels. Let them dry until you are certain no water remains on them at all.

4. Place fruit on a parchment-lined cookie sheet, being careful that none of the fruit touches each other, and freeze overnight.

5. Place frozen fruit in a plastic freezer bag.

6. Use a straw as a vacuum to suck out as much air as possible.

7. Place the DIY vacuum-sealed fruit bag into another freezer bag and label it. The double bag method discourages freezer burn.

Note about freezing vegetables:

Before freezing, vegetables require the additional step of blanching to further slow enzymatic activity and keep color, texture, flavor, and nutritional value intact. To blanch most vegetables, dunk them into rapidly boiling water for three minutes (two minutes for tender greens). Immediately after boiling, plunge vegetables in an ice-water bath to stop the cooking. Cut blanched vegetables into uniform pieces and follow steps 3–7 for freezing fruit.

DRYING

This is the oldest form of preservation and another very easy way to save the goodies you've grown. Drying (or dehydrating) doesn't keep the original texture intact but it adds a new, interesting one. The process concentrates the sugars, resulting a pleasantly rubbery chew. Another advantage to drying is saving space since dried fruits and vegetables hardly take up any room. Once you start drying your harvest, you'll wonder why you didn't do it with foods from the market. Homemade spices, soups, and trail mixes elevate front yard food to a whole new level of fun.

Unlike canning and jarring, which have rigid rules and regulations to ensure against the growth of potentially lethal toxins, drying can be done without too much anxiety. The main thing to worry about is humidity—never a friend to the home dryer—spoiling your goods. Without investing in a costly dehydrator, you can still experiment with three drying methods.

Air. If you have a dry corner of your home, you can hang herbs and edible flowers to air dry. Wrap them loosely in cheesecloth to discourage dust from collecting on your future pantry spices. Next, tie the stems together tightly with rubber bands (which will hold the stems fast as they shrink from loss of water) and hang the bundles upside down. Check them every few days—when they are crunchy you can crumble them or grind with a mortar and pestle. Store dried goods in airtight jars.

Oven. This method is especially easy if your oven has a convection setting. If it doesn't, put your oven on its lowest setting and leave the door slightly ajar to let humidity escape. After washing, slice your fruits or vegetable into thin pieces. Place them on parchment-lined cookie sheets, and leave them in the oven until they are thoroughly dry to the touch. This usually takes several hours. Depending on how you want to use your dried food, you can stop at the chewy, slightly rubbery stage (dried fruit for trail mixes) or you can dehydrate even further to make dried veggie snacks or vegetable powders. After you dry and powder onions and garlic, your spice rack will never be the same.

Sun. Sun drying takes a long time—usually 4 or 5 days with very low humidity and temperatures above 90 degrees. Getting the right conditions can be frustrating for even the most dedicated. If you do have the right conditions and really want the romance of authentically sundried tomatoes, I won't try and discourage you. Spread your thinly sliced garden treasures onto a window screen (you may have to invest in a new one) to keep the warm air circulating. Place the screen in full sun every morning and bring it in at night. Once you've achieved that perfect sundried tomato, rejoice. (Another hint: don't put the screen near any known bird hangout. One bird dropping fiasco could ruin days of patient effort and thoroughly gross you out.)

share and share alike

At the beginning of the gardening season, all of us are a little stingy. We want to relish everything we grow, cook it with our own hands, and serve it to our families and friends. This will likely change as summer progresses. Sometimes, you will have so much food that you don't even want to take the time to save it for winter—you just need to get it out of your kitchen as fast as possible. Friends of gardeners come to expect and look forward to receiving the glut of a good year (unless perhaps they're getting zucchini for the tenth time).

But there may come a time when even your friends don't know what to do with the produce from your edible garden gone wild. This is when you share with the world. Local food pantries, churches, and homeless shelters would love your bounty. More than just being fun, sharing cuttings, seeds, and food is a gardener's duty. Our forefathers did this because they knew that one day, in the event of a crop failure, they might need some of those seeds, a cutting of a plant, or a basket of food themselves. It is part of being neighborly and connecting to the community, and an important part of what gardening—especially in the front yard—is all about.

....

OPPOSITE: Share your garden bounty with friends, neighbors, and strangers. Photo by Ann Summa

getting ready for next time

Seasons come and seasons go. No matter how much productivity and beauty you want to squeeze out of your front yard, sometimes it needs a little tender loving care. Just think of everything your front yard edible garden gave you during the growing season. Even in climates where the growing season is extended, take a little time to clean things up, straighten things out, and replenish the soil that has been so good to you.

CLEANING UP AND COMPOSTING

Nothing in the garden goes to waste. Even plants that weren't very productive will add to the overall health of next season's garden if they end up in the compost pile. Pull out annual crops by the roots and examine them before composting. Don't compost anything that is diseased or mildewy—plant-borne diseases will spread through the compost to the next year's crops.

In areas with mild winters, cut back perennial crops to encourage a better shape and fresh growth. In cold winter areas, you can wait until spring to cut back most of the perennials—the dead foliage behaves as a buffer against the cold.

After harvesting and cutting, it's time to add fresh compost to your garden. If the soil level in raised beds has dropped considerably, replenish it now. If you cut back evergreen and perennial plants, top dress the soil in between them with at least two inches of compost, and cover that with a generous helping of dried leaves as mulch. You can either plant a fall/winter edible garden in your freshly composted garden, or allow the compost and mulch to sit and revitalize the soil until the following spring.

COVER CROPS

Planting a cover crop (a plant that enhances the quality of soil) in your edible beds is a smart option for winter. It saves beds from looking empty while simultaneously preparing the soil for next season's edible bonanza. Clover, winter rye, and mustards are all good choices for cover crops. Sow seeds thickly, and in the spring till the young, fresh crop back into the soil as a "green manure." Another popular cover crop is fava beans. Favas are super nitrogen-fixers, which means they give nitrogen back to the soil in a way next year's plants can use. After a season of intensive food growing, your depleted soil will love you for planting a cover crop that returns some of that nourishment—and you'll get fava beans as a bonus. Seed companies sell a certain type of fava beans especially for use as a cover crop, but since all favas have this nitrogen fixing ability I'd recommend going with the yummy variety of your choice. Compost the bean foliage instead of tilling it back into the beds and your soil will be ready for another season of abundant growth.

GOODNIGHT, BEDS

If you live in a freeze zone and you won't be planting a winter garden or cover crop, put your edible garden to bed by composting your beds and borders, then piling up a generous mulch of dried leaves around the crowns of your perennials. This extra mulch gives a cushion of protection against the coming cold which your plants will appreciate. Some gardeners who are trying to grow plants that are too tender for their zone will bind their roses and shrubs into burlap forms. If done well, wrapping plants with burlap can blend into the browns, grays, barks, and dried leaves of the winter landscape.

....

OPPOSITE: Chard is a fabulous and hardy edible. Photo by Ann Summa

winter gardens

Fall and winter are great times to garden—if the climate is right. Determine the germination and growth rates of your desired crops, count backwards from your first estimated frost date, and plant your winter edibles accordingly. In frost-free zones, you can plant all year long and enjoy the rougher, textural look of the winter garden, with its cabbages and kales. Take every opportunity to bring color into this leaf-heavy season of gardening: Russian and lacinato kale, 'Bright Lights' chard, red mustards, and the marvelous 'Bull's Blood' beets will brighten things up. Your front yard can have almost as much interest during the "fallow" season as it does during the traditional growing season.

EDIBLES FOR WINTER INTEREST

- Beets
- Chard
- Fava beans
- Garlic
- Kale
- Lettuce
- Mustard
- Onions
- Peas
- Spinach

STRETCH YOUR SEASON

Many gardeners utilize plastic-covered hoop structures to extend their growing season, but I think front yard gardeners have to draw the aesthetic line somewhere— our front yard edible gardens shouldn't look like nurseries. If you garden in a cold zone and want to extend your season, use cloches and cold frames. A cloche is a small, transparent covering (often made of glass) that will protect individual plants from the cold. A cold frame is a small greenhouse-like structure that is built low to the ground; it usually has a hinged glass roof. These will integrate into your hardscape better than large, unwieldy structures that interfere with the design you've created. You have worked hard to build a space that looks good from season to season—find the solution to keeping your winter crops warm that's as attractive as the rest of your garden.

TAKE A BREATHER

A front yard winter garden can be an active growing space or a period of rest and revitalization. A well-planned garden will have the necessary structural support, in both plants and hardscape, to carry it through this quiet time of the gardening year. A winter garden is beautiful and should be appreciated; you don't need to feel the pressure to grow grow grow all year long. Or perhaps it's simply impossible. If it is cold and unforgiving outside, do what gardeners for generations have done—sit inside by a fire with a hot cup of tea and a stack of seed catalogues. Start dreaming about next spring. Put extra stars by the edibles with interesting colors, forms, and textures. Soon you'll be itching to get back out there and expand on what you've learned.

you did it!

You've done something big. You've transformed a common, everyday front lawn into an edible oasis: a vibrant, colorful, interesting model of what a front yard can be. By taking this chance in the most public, visible place on your property, you've shouted "I care" loud and clear to everyone who passes by. You care enough about our natural resources to get rid of a thirsty patch of sod and replace it with a garden, a mini Eden. You care enough about yourself and your family to take the time to grow food, and to do so organically.

With a few simple principles of garden design, you've created a space that's redefining curb appeal. You've saved the edible garden from the shadows of the back yard. It's now standing proud in the sunlight, where it belongs, reflecting your personal style and passions. Congratulations on your deliciously beautiful new adventure. It will get better every season. Now go eat some of your front yard food!

OPPOSITE, TOP: The clean, chunky hardscape, and the integrated mix of well-selected ornamentals, provides a framework to grow seasonal edibles, harvest them, and have the front yard look great all year long. Photo by Ann Summa. Garden of Yvette Roman and Fred Davis

OPPOSITE, BOTTOM: A summer morning's harvest from my edible front yard. Photo by Ivette Soler

references & resources

HELPFUL READING

Haeg, Fritz. *Edible Estates: Attack on the Front Lawn.* Los Angeles, California: Metropolis Books, 2008

Kingsolver, Barbara. *Animal, Vegetable, Miracle: A Year of Food Life.* New York: HarperCollins, 2008.

McLaughlin, Chris. *The Complete Idiot's Guide to Composting.* New York: Alpha/Penguin, 2010.

Pollan, Michael. *The Omnivore's Dilemma: A Natural History of Four Meals.* New York: Penguin Press, 2006.

Van Krevelen, Jean Ann, Amanda Thomsen, Teresa O'Connor, and Robin Ripley. *Grocery Gardening: Planting, Preparing and Preserving Fresh Food.* Brentwood, Tennessee: Cool Springs Press, 2010.

Editors of Sunset Books. *Western Garden Book of Edibles: The Complete A–Z Guide to Growing Your Own Vegetables, Herbs, and Fruits.* Menlo Park, California: Sunset Publishing, 2010.

SEED RESOURCES

Annie's Annuals & Perennials
801 Chesley Avenue
Richmond, CA 94801
1.888.266.4370
www.anniesannuals.com

Fedco Seeds
PO Box 520
Waterfield, ME 04903
207.873.7333
www.fedcoseeds.com

Seed Saver's Exchange
3094 North Wynn Road
Decorah, IA 52101
563.382.5990
www.seedsavers.org

Baker Creek Heirloom Seeds
2278 Baker Creek Road
Mansfield, MO 65704
417.924.8917
www.rareseeds.com

Johnny's Selected Seeds
955 Benton Avenue
Winslow, ME 04901
877.564.6697
www.johnnyseeds.com

Territorial Seed Company
PO Box 158
Cottage Grove, OR 97424
800-626-0866
www.territorialseeds.com

Burpee
W. Atlee Burpee & Co.
300 Park Avenue
Warminster, PA 18974
724.263.0363
www.burpee.com

Plant Delights Nursery, Inc.
9241 Sauls Road
Raleigh, NC 27603
919.722.4794
www.plantdelights.com

Yucca Do Nursery, Inc.
PO Box 1039
Giddings, TX 78942
979.542.8811
www.yuccado.com

OPPOSITE: Feverfew whispers gently to lime thyme "We look great together." Photo by Ann Summa

index

about the author

Ivette Soler is a garden designer and writer living in Los Angeles, California. Her plant design work for Elysian Landscapes, and her own personal garden, have appeared in magazines such as *Metropolitan Home, Sunset,* and *House & Garden,* as well as in several books. Ivette's garden writing has been featured in *Garden Design, Cottage Living,* and *Budget Living,* and she was the resident gardening expert on NBC's *The Bonnie Hunt Show.* Her popular gardening blog, The Germinatrix, originated in 2006 as part of *Domino* magazine; since 2009, Ivette's blog has been thriving independently at www.thegerminatrix.com.